Granddad's Dictionary

Reflections on life in America

MICHAEL MOFFITT

WESTBOW·
PRESS
A DIVISION OF THOMAS NELSON
& ZONDERVAN

WestBow Press books may be ordered through booksellers or by contacting:

WestBow Press
A Division of Thomas Nelson & Zondervan
1663 Liberty Drive
Bloomington, IN 47403
www.westbowpress.com
1 (866) 928-1240

Quote on page 123, paragraph 3 (Matthew 7:12) from
The Jerusalem Bible, Doubleday, 1966.

ISBN: 978-1-4908-2916-6 (sc)
ISBN: 978-1-4908-2917-3 (hc)
ISBN: 978-1-4908-2915-9 (e)

Library of Congress Control Number: 2014904190

Printed in the United States of America.

WestBow Press rev. date: 04/04/2014

Contents

Dedicated to
Marion and Roy
Who gave me life and taught me how to live it

Introduction

One of the advantages of being a granddad is that you have experienced the passage of at least three generations and have participated in several cycles of economic and national life. You have made more mistakes and hopefully accumulated some wisdom that is less apparent to younger generations. This book began as an effort to pass along these lessons and to build a stronger bridge to my grandchildren. As it evolved and its scope expanded, many have encouraged sharing it with a larger audience.

Granddad's Dictionary is a collection of reflections on the history and values that made America exceptional. Many of these reflections also articulate lessons vital to the sustenance of our freedom and our way of life in the twenty first century.

The book is organized around words. Each word educes some reflections, thoughts and memories. Some are philosophical. Some are personal. Some are practical. Each word and the associated reflections stand on their own. The reflections can be read in any sequence, but they are not independent or unrelated. There are two complimentary themes that emerge, more from the flow of my thoughts than a result of some planned organization. Both have a common origin, an immense gratitude for being born at my time and place and in the home of my parents. Both also reflect a concern that the values underlying the foundation for that great opportunity are eroding and that the prospect for my grandchildren to have such a fullness of good fortune are less than fully assured.

The first theme is our parents and their parents' unqualified respect for, and and faith in the potential of every citizen, a respect and faith that we forsake at our peril. This is imbedded in our nation's founding fathers' vision, and it is also personal. If we expect to carry forward the vision of freedom, we must live our lives according to its principles and aspirations.

The second theme follows from the first. Our political fulcrum too frequently is the last crisis or the next election and too seldom the next generations. As a result we are at risk to embed already obsolete micro-managed solutions for every contemporary problem. These solutions are often motivated by expectation of the least wisdom and worst behavior rather than the best possible from our citizenry. The underlying expectations, whatever they may be, tend to create their own reality.

Maintaining high expectations is not a naïve dream. It is a necessary condition for the survival of a free people. Failure to do so is not something we can blame on politicians or political parties. My hope is that my grandchildren and whoever else reads these reflections will as a result demand higher standards from themselves and a longer and broader perspective from their leaders.

Several of the reflections suggest policy alternatives, but these are not inflexible or partisan. Granddad does not dictate recipes or answers. Rather, this is a book of questions, riddles and challenges to individuals about themselves, their values, our civilization and our future.

Accountability

It is not written in natural law that any person or group of people is wiser or more righteous than any other. It is natural and universal human behavior that each of us selfishly seeks the power and resources to fulfill our needs, desires and dreams. Each of us has a sense of what is right and seeks to impose that right on those around us. Anyone who questions this truth only needs look at the behavior of small children.

Lord Acton, renowned nineteenth century historian and moralist coined the famous adage, "Absolute power corrupts absolutely." That phrase is elegant in its simplicity. The power we seek, by its nature, is not subject to accountability. To the extent we are accountable our power is limited. To the extent we are not accountable, we lose track of the line between others' versions of "right" and our own. We should note that the adage is absolute in its truth for all people. It does not say, "Power especially corrupts presidents or senators or bankers," nor does it offer an exemption to ministers, teachers, workers or children.

Corruption clogs the productive machinery of cooperative endeavors. History is the witness that most civilizations eventually are plagued by corruption, and that corruption is invariably a seed of their ultimate collapse. Accountability is the lubricant that removes the friction of corruption and keeps a civilization functioning smoothly. Accountability is the demanded acceptance of responsibility for our actions and commitments. Without a commitment to accountability, there is no integrity and there can be no trust.

Three conditions are necessary and sufficient to preserve accountability. None of these has to do with men and women of great character, as there are too few saints among us. The first and most difficult condition is a common set of values. Without shared values we are unlikely to reach a shared concept of accountability. The second condition is transparency. The best test of ethical behavior is a willingness to read about our activities in the morning paper. The final requirement is the distribution of power... checks and balances, so that for every concentration of power, there are offsetting concentrations to provide balance and to enforce transparency and consequences. Each of these is embedded in America's DNA. Each will be a recurring theme in Granddad's reflections.

Activists

When I was a young man I was active in the movement to control printing presses with computers. We created many innovations. One resulted in saving three trees out of each one hundred needed to print magazines. I was an inventor in the development of on line shopping. My team created an Amazon.com like experience in a kiosk in 1987, one year after Jeff Bezos was graduated from Princeton and seven years before he founded Amazon.com. I was an inventor and a pioneer in the movement to create text and image databases that enabled customized publishing and provided the backbone for interactive publishing.

Nobody has ever called me an activist for any of these activities. Contemporary vernacular does not recognize them as activism. Webster defines activism as, "A doctrine or practice that emphasizes direct vigorous action, especially in support of or opposition to one side of a controversial issue."

Perhaps to be an activist, one needs to be a critic, to marshal emotions and resources for good things or against bad things or bad people. An activist may be for equality, justice, preservation or sustainability or against greed, corruption, pollution, injustice, inequality, big government, or any bad thing. The activist emphasizes political action in support of or against an issue. Activism is measured by polemic and noise. Its product is awareness and its goal is frequently political change. The activist is by definition swimming upstream, against the grain, because the controversial issue is not yet resolved.

If you are for something and working to effect positive change through the marketplace, you must be more than an activist. You must be an inventor, a reformer, an entrepreneur, a builder, an executive and a producer, working to satisfy needs and creating value in the eyes of investors and customers. The producer may not like aspects of the environment he works in and may agree with the activist's mission, but the focus is different.

Activists remind us of our inconsistencies and infirmities. Activism may be a heroic and Sisyphean endeavor. The desired result is to change the status quo or resolve a cultural or political issue, even though such things are seldom resolved with finality. Yet we should not canonize the idealism of the activist. Usually, where there is controversy, there is merit on both sides. The activist is not necessarily wiser or better informed or purer of heart than those who do not share the mission. The producers, those who work within the existing environment and know its strengths and shortcomings should converse with the activist. The activist should also listen and be dedicated to becoming a producer. We all should realize that it is the producers who create the innovation and wealth that give the activist the luxury to criticize.

Perhaps the greatest dilemma is that faced by the activist educator. The educator's responsibility is to teach critical thinking and analysis of problems and issues from various and often conflicting perspectives. The activist's mission is to act on or support one side of an issue, ignoring or suppressing counterpoints. The conflict of interest is daunting. Ironically, this lesson is lost on many professors who regard themselves as both educators and activists.

American Exceptionalism

How is it that a remote and unorganized land populated largely by adventurers, paupers, criminals, religious castaways, indentured servants and slaves became the richest and most powerful nation in the world, perhaps in the history of the world, in less than 200 years? How could this upstart surpass colonial powers that controlled and extracted resources far beyond their borders and become the savior of homelands to those previously great but now weakened empires?

Emerson best expressed the answer in *Self-Reliance*. "There is a time in every man's education when he arrives at the conviction that envy is ignorance; that imitation is suicide; that he must take himself for better, for worse, as his portion; that though the wide universe is full of good, no kernel of nourishing corn can come to him but through his toil bestowed on that plot of ground which is given to him to till."

Few citizens of the United States during its first 150 years believed that anyone, especially government owed citizens anything other than liberty and opportunity as protected in the Bill of Rights. So the citizens, not all of them but enough, used that liberty to exploit opportunity. Inherent in this process was an appetite for risk, willingness, even a necessity to take risks and to accept that he who takes the risks is accountable for both the winnings and the losses. The consequences were great innovation, many fortunes made and lost and a culture of personal responsibility. More important was a culture of respect for personal accomplishment, a sense that every citizen has the opportunity to raise his or her station in life and in which classes have no boundaries or barriers.

Add to this culture a market economy where customers are deemed the wisest judges of the value of goods and services. Citizens as customers determine worth by their willingness to purchase or not to purchase at the price asked. Add a willingness to share our values by welcoming of the world's huddled masses with the only condition being that they join the culture of self-reliance.

A second answer, famously articulated by President John F. Kennedy, was a culture of service. "Ask not what your country can do for you, ask what you can do for your country." At our founding, civil service was a civil responsibility. There were no career legislators or politicians. It was thought one should be a taxpayer to vote and be successful within the community before representing the community in government. There were volunteer firefighters, mayors and councilmen. Workers in the public sector were thought of by all as "public servants," and they were typically paid less than those in the private sector if at all. There were no public employee unions or pensions. In the 1920s, 150 years after our founding and with a history that included civil war, a brutal world war and numerous financial panics, the nation's budget and federal debt were each about three percent of the annual income produced within the nation. All these are reasons that America became truly exceptional.

In 1941, after 165 years of national life and eight years of world financial collapse and depression, America had the resources and the national will to save the democratic world from being overrun by despots. No nation in human history has ever fought a war so unselfishly. Nor has any other nation rebuilt its devastated allies and conquered foes with such generosity. That was the finest moment of American Exceptionalism.

American Exceptionalism should not be mistaken for American perfection. Perhaps most exceptional is that Americans recognize imperfections, dedicate themselves to fixing them and to answering any threat. We do this through checks and balances on power. Not just administrative vs. judicial vs. legislative power but also federal vs. state & local governments vs. free market power. We ended slavery, tamed cartels, created new institutions to provide safety nets for the most needy, removed economic and social barriers for laborers, minorities and women, fought two world wars against global oppression and are fighting another against terrorism. The process of making ourselves better and stronger is not perfect and not easy, but we as a nation have always done so with vigor.

We now face a threat of our own making. We have planted the seeds of our own destruction. We have a self-inflicted infection that is sapping our vitality and our Exceptionalism. That infection is debt!

Today, our national debt is over $17 trillion, more than $55 thousand per man woman and child. Our debt has surpassed our annual national income. There is no projection and no apparent will for it to be reduced. This immodest number does not include actuarial shortages in the Social Security Trust Fund or liabilities for government insured mortgages. Add a few trillion more. Federal expenditures at $4 trillion are eight times the share of our income as on our 150th birthday, more than $12 thousand per man woman and child and 25 percent more than Federal revenues. For the moment, we have artificially low interest rates, held down by "monetary easing." Inevitably, we will return to normal or higher than normal rates of inflation and interest. By 2018, with the projected debt at 20 trillion dollars and three percent or more inflation, our interest bill will be the largest line item in the federal budget. It will be larger than Social Security, larger than defense and larger than Medicare. Someone else will have to save the world from the next despot or from global terrorism or global warming or from whatever crisis one can imagine. We no longer have the financial resources.

American Exceptionalism is no longer supported by our national policy. It still exists in our DNA, and in many of our lives. It is, however at great risk of being frittered away by those who no longer remember our history and take no responsibility for debt. If we decide to pass this debt to our children, we will have consumed our exceptional birthright and given them shackles in its place.

Ante

An Ante is the price you pay to get into a game or an opportunity. At the poker table, a higher ante builds the pot faster, makes the winnings bigger, and also keeps those with the least capital out of the game.

In 1994 when the minimum wage was $5.25 per hour, I bought and began to run a printing company. We had many minimum wage employees handling valuable and time sensitive product and working with expensive and complicated equipment. It was apparent that prior management believed too much that low wages were a good thing. In order to focus the supervisory team on quality and skills, we issued an edict that no employee who was not worth at least eight dollars per hour was qualified to be on our team. Each employee currently below that rate was put on a program to learn to perform at a level worth, and to be paid, at least eight dollars per hour within one year, or be dismissed. Most people succeeded. Our turnover went down, quality and productivity improved. A few employees did not succeed and were dismissed. Because productivity had improved, not all of those were replaced.

In our case, raising the "minimum wage" was good for our customers who received better quality and service. It was good for our costs and our profits. It was good for the employees who earned higher wages. It was **not** good for the few who lost their jobs or for others who applied and could not meet new and higher standards. We had raised the ante, raised the winnings for those in the game and excluded those with the least ability to play.

So it is with any increase in the minimum wage or minimum requirements for participation in any activity. Licensing, qualifying tests, entrance standards, union membership or apprenticeships all can raise requirements of the population allowed to enter an activity. Just as any ante they make the activity more exclusive, more profitable and frequently improve quality. The cost for all these benefits is borne by those who cannot afford the ante or pass the screen to get into the game. This is neither good nor bad. It is simply the way the world is. Antes of all sorts raise standards and at the same time provide a harsh incentive for those who aspire to meet a higher bar to get into the game.

Arrogance

Arrogance is a learning disability. One who already knows everything, or thinks that he does, has lost all thirst and incentive for learning. Without a measure of humility, we cannot recognize opportunities to learn or to reach for higher levels of performance. No matter how good we become, none of our lives or works are without flaw or without the opportunity to seek greater perfection. No matter how much we know, there is no one from whom we have nothing to learn. Arrogance and hubris are life-limiting failures to grasp this fundamental truth.

Art

The languages of sub-Saharan Africans and Native Americans do not contain an equivalent to our word art! Those peoples had no equivalent to our concept of Art. All the things we look at as art from these cultures were created for a human purpose. Perhaps they were spiritual symbols or tools of courtship, or marks of identity, or decorations. Perhaps they were art as we would define it, but the concept of art was not part of the creator's vernacular.

We have progressed in our artistic sensibility to a point where art is now a huge commercial enterprise. Thousands of artists make their living, or try to, by producing stuff people will buy as art. Good art is often defined as marketable art. Our collective sense of discrimination seems dulled, willing to accept many things as art that require little creativity or craftsmanship and serve no human function, things that justify themselves only as cool, or startling or vulgar creations attracting attention or stimulating the senses. We sometimes must wonder if our more primitive antecedents had a better standard of artistic value.

We think of art differently than manufactured products. Aspects of any product design may include style or beauty, but the driving force is to achieve the desired function at a marketable cost. Perfection is not a requirement or even necessarily a goal. Meeting the specification is good enough. Any deviation by definition does not add value. Better than "good enough" can be "too good", especially when it comes at a cost.

In art, "good enough" is the enemy of perfection and thus the enemy of success. A work of art can be a painting, a sculpture, a photograph, literature, music, dance, a garden, a building, a design, or an expression in any media, or even a life. The standard of perfection is subjective and individual. To qualify as art, the work must only be a worthy result of a creative and experimental process in pursuit of perfection. The value of a work of art has no relationship to its cost or to the opinion of the artist. Its value lies in the response it educes from observers.

It is a great mistake to be rigid in the judgment of art. If it awes or stimulates a new feeling or idea, then that is to be relished. It is instructive to ask, "Why do I value this experience more or less than others?" Every viewing of a work of art is a test for both the artist and the viewer.

What better way could there be to teach unique life skills to young children than to teach them about Art? They can start with very simple skills, set their own goals, develop and test their own concepts and continue to raise aspirations as their skills and confidence grow. Encourage them to enjoy seeking their own perfection. Let them test their response to creations of others. Do the same for yourself.

Bureaucrats

Customers reward the entrepreneur for creating value. Value is measured by profit, created when the entrepreneur's cost to produce a good or service is less than the value the customer assigns by the price he pays. Profit adds to the entrepreneur's wealth and to the wealth of the whole community. In every transaction every day, the entrepreneur has that "value added" as a measure of his performance. Without value added, his product is not worth what it costs and the market will quickly punish him.

The bureaucrat has the luxury of confusing motion with performance. If he shows up and does what he feels is good, he sees himself as good.

Although we frequently think of bureaucrats in government, there are many bureaucrats in the private sector. Typically, however, they are judged by their contribution to the enterprise and to creation of value. Bureaucrats in the private sector, even in the non-profit private sector ultimately have to satisfy customers or they do not survive. The crucible of customer satisfaction at a profit is an unforgiving regimen.

In government, however, power is embedded into the bureau, and the bureaucrat has the ability to expand his role and his budget and his power without the consent of any customers. When he does, he usurps the power of decisions from the public and from the market. Alexis deTocqueville, a French political thinker and author of *Democracy in America* predicted this possibility for America early in the nineteenth century. James Buchannan saw it as well.

Michael Moffitt

James Buchannan, economist and namesake of our fifteenth president won the 1986 Nobel Prize for Economics for his work studying how politicians' self-interest and non-economic forces affect government policy. He argued and demonstrated the obvious, that politicians and government officials — like other participants in an economic system — act in their own self-interest. Since the policymakers' goal is to be re-elected or to maintain or expand his or her power, they do not always act in the best interest of the public. Buchannan observed that bureaucracies do not behave benevolently. They expand exponentially and create more demands than they satisfy.

Isn't that amazing! Not his findings, but that such obvious findings could justify a Nobel Prize. Nineteen eighty-six must have been a weak year for the dismal science. It is not news that each of us seeks power to control and continuously improve our self-interest. It would be absurd to suggest that any person or group of people consistently act against their own self-interest or willingly cede their personal power. In government, the bureaucrat is too far removed from the customer to realistically be subjected to accountability.

Our founding fathers knew this. That is why they created tension between Executive, Legislative and Judicial branches, and between Federal and State Governments and the people. That is why they reserved for the people all powers not specifically given to the government in the Constitution. That is why Jefferson was fonder of the Declaration of Independence than of the Constitution.

14

Charity

For the first 150 years of our great Republic charity was left largely to individuals, churches, families, neighbors, relief organizations and perhaps to local militia or municipal government. Charity was viewed as personal and civic responsibility, not a function of the State. It was a given that many, including rich and poor, tithed; they gave 10 percent of their income to those they could help.

It is not so today! Beginning in the great depression, we nationalized charity. As with any national priority or responsibility, we sweep with a very wide broom. Today we spend 10 percent of our national income to support Social Security, Medicare, unemployment and federal welfare programs. Most of this started as charity but much has evolved into income re-distribution disguised as insurance.

We think that government encourages private giving with tax deductions, but we should think more carefully. A tax deduction for me requires an increase in your taxes to pay for what my taxes would have bought if I did not get the deduction. So when Bill Gates or Warren Buffett or your favorite rock star or NFL quarterback creates a foundation, everyone else pays the 40 cents of every dollar or more to fund their tax deduction. Today there are over 1.5 million non-profit organizations in the United States, including churches, temples, mosques, schools, hospitals, research groups, advocacy groups, domestic and international relief groups, think tanks, private foundations, museums, and the like. Every person in America can find some things good or favorable on this list, and some not. We all finance other peoples tax deductions on all charities indiscriminately, in addition to our own giving.

This process is loved and defended by almost everyone, even though it is wasteful and corrupt. It funds competing interests while depriving taxpayers the freedom to not give to some or any. It gives private foundations the license to maintain control of taxpayers' money, grow it without paying taxes on the gains, use it to fund administrative costs including salaries and travel expenses for self and family and distribute it where and when they please. All this would be fine if people freely gave their own after tax funds. Our indiscriminate tax subsidy for private foundations is as silly as having renters of apartments and small houses subsidize tax deductions on interest and taxes for owners of larger and more expensive homes.

Some believe that giving would be reduced without the tax subsidy, but history does not support that belief. Before income taxes we had foundations, we had Churches hospitals asylums and private schools, we had the Red Cross and the Salvation Army and Carnegie Libraries and we had tithing. We should ask, "Do we as a people today give two percent of our income to charity because of a tax deduction incentive, or do we give only two percent because so much responsibility and so many of the fruits of our labor have been usurped by the public sector?"

Perhaps the most heartbreaking aspect of government charity and charitable tax subsidies is the distance they put between the donor and the recipient. The closer we are to a problem, the more we participate in the solution, not just with money, but also as individual human beings. The closer we are to the charitable organization the more time we give and the more discipline and responsiveness we require from its leaders. We cannot turn back the clock in an instant, but clearly all movement away from government charity puts every donor closer to those being helped and increases our freedom to choose in a free market for good works.

Christianity

All religions have a spiritual aspect, teachings about God and Man's relationship to God. They also have a cultural aspect, the impact of the religion and those who practice it on civilization and on their fellow man. Both are important and instructive when reflecting on Christianity or on any religion. I am a Christian, but my relationship to God is a personal matter. In this reflection, the focus is on the impact of Christianity on our civilization.

The awesome impact of Christianity on human civilization is inescapable. Christian investment was a major force in art, architecture, music, philosophy and organization for centuries, at least through the dawn of the Industrial Revolution. It is not a coincidence that the Renaissance first flourished in Italy, facilitated by the wealth and power of the Roman Catholic Church. Florence, the epicenter of the Renaissance, was home to Michelangelo and Leonardo da Vinci. The first great works of Renaissance architecture were cathedrals, including the Church of Saint Andrew in Mantua and Saint Peter's Basilica. Paintings of religious and biblical scenes were dominant as subjects of Renaissance art.

Think also of the music of worship by Bach, Barstow, Bortnainsky, Castellanos, Handel, Praetorius or any of a multitude of classical composers of Christian music, and the thousands who played and listened to their music. Reflect on the hundreds of thousands of singers, musicians, instrument makers and teachers in churches over the centuries. Where would they have found their training or a fertile market without Christianity?

Medieval philosophy was characteristically theological. Most medieval thinkers did not consider themselves philosophers at all. Their concerns were theological. The Reformation in the sixteenth century and the enlightenment period beginning in the late seventeenth century built on that theological foundation, promoting humanism, science and intellectual interchange while opposing intolerance and abuses by church and state. America's founding fathers were not all churchmen and had widely different religious practices, but nearly all shared the Christian vocabulary and used it in expressing the founding principles of our nation. Undeniably our freedoms would have been crafted very differently without this Christian heritage.

The first book to be printed using movable type was the Bible. It is also the most printed and most read document in the history of mankind. For at least two centuries in Europe, more people learned to read reading the Bible than all other books. The impact of mass availability of the Bible on literacy is immeasurable.

The Vatican was the first organization model for international corporations, managing a worldwide enterprise within the constraints of the laws and culture of each of its host nations.

All this is history. It does not require or support a judgment that Christian governance, doctrine or beliefs are good or bad, fact or myth. It should, however, make us pause that one humble and powerless being and his radical message of humility, forgiveness and hope and those who have subscribed to His message have had so much positive impact on human civilization two millennia later. Can it be argued that any other being in history has approached that influence?

In this same history, Christian crusades and Christian states have been oppressive, murderous and corrupt in their pursuit of converts and wealth and power. Yet Christian institutions have reformed themselves from the inside and continue to do so. The message of Jesus has resonated with and has been preserved by believers with sufficient strength to tame popes and kings and to purify their own institutions. Perhaps this is the greatest testament to the power of the Christian message, and the integrity and courage of those who honor it.

Michael Moffitt

Civilization

Civilization is the result of our distant ancestors pooling their interests. When man was a wandering hunter he lived only by his individual wit. If he could not survive by his wit alone, he perished. When man became a farmer and formed communities, he improved his chances. The community profited by division of labor and survived by its collective wit.

A civilization is the sum of all the culture, ideas, innovations, ethics, organization and physical assets of a people. It is the collective wit of its citizens and their ancestors and all the resulting assets.

Alfred North Whitehead described: "Civilization advances by extending the number of important operations we can perform without thinking about them." The more advanced a civilization becomes, the more intelligence and assets it possesses and the better the possibilities for its entire people. A greater collective wit and more important operations performed without having to think about them benefit all people.

In our civilization we drive a car, make a phone call, watch television, use a computer, take a vacation, eat in a restaurant, invest our savings, all without the need to understand in detail the art or science or skills required to make these activities possible. We have the opportunity to follow the news, secure an education, enjoy the possibilities of medicine and protection of law; all without understanding how these opportunities are provided. The ability to benefit from many things we do not understand gives us the opportunity to specialize and be more productive in those things we like or do best. The more information we have available, the lesser proportion each of us can master and the more we can and must specialize. One gets a sense of the pace of this development in our civilization from the discipline of medicine. In less than a century we have migrated from nurses, midwives and doctors to hundreds of specialized therapists and concentrations within the fields of nursing and medicine. Today one almost never hears of a doctor without a specialty. No single individual can master the scope of all medical practice. The same is true of engineers, lawyers, architects, and even accountants.

The word "civilization" was first used in the eighteenth century. It derives from the Latin civis, meaning citizen and civitis, meaning city or city-state. Arnold Toynbee studied the rise and fall of twenty-one civilizations in *A Study of History* published from 1934 to 1961. Toynbee's conclusion in *Civilizations on Trial* was, "Civilizations, I believe, come to birth and proceed to grow by successfully responding to successive challenges. They break down and go to pieces if and when a challenge confronts them which they fail to meet." Toynbee describes, as have many others, the most important aspect of all civilizations is their dynamism. The world is never static. Success is never permanent. The future is impossible to predict. The most important quality of any civilization, including our own, is its creative ability to respond to unexpected challenge and change.

The United States is arguably the most creative, most prosperous and most generous nation in the history of mankind. Those of us here today had little to do with creating this great heritage. If we accept responsibility to pass it along to following generations, our mission must not be to make things easier, or to keep things the same or even to solve a particular contemporary problem. Our mission must be above all else to preserve and enhance future generations' ability to respond to unexpected challenge and change. To fulfill this mission it is essential to understand the process of evolution of civilizations. For lack of a better word, I call this process "civilution".

Civilution

I was unable to find a word that denotes the organic evolutionary and revolutionary process of the growth and dissolution of civilizations, so I made up the word "Civilution."

When Henry Ford and Ransom Olds built the first automobile assembly lines, could they have conceived of an automobile industry remotely like the one we know today?

When John Barber patented the first turbine in 1791, could he or could the Wright brothers a century later have conceived the modern aircraft and air transportation industries? Gordon Moore surmised in 1965 that the power of integrated circuits would double every two years, as it had for the previous eight, at least until 1975. Who could have conceived this prediction would still be working and celebrated as "Moore's Law" fifty years later? Who could lead the symphony of innovation multiplying upon innovation constantly reinventing our way of life and creating a vast array of new products, new wealth and new experiences? Who could even design an effective set of incentives that might assure this constant and repeating transformation? Why is it that, since it's founding America has been the most powerful cradle of innovation in the history of the world?

Each of us knows only a miniscule portion of the vast array of information available to us, but each of us knows a different portion. Every new idea is the product of old ideas in a new context. Many people saw apples fall from trees before Newton grasped the concept of gravity. Study of bird's wings and bicycle manufacture came together at Kitty Hawk to solve the millennia old riddle of man's flight. Each discovery or new idea is a collision of information in a human mind that sees it in a new way. Each innovation is largely an accidental discovery of a new piece to a larger puzzle. Each of these accidental ideas is a small step in civilution, in the creative development of civilization.

Can there be a seer who predicts the output of a new idea or who can predict what other new idea will result from it? Can there be an arbiter of the creative process capable of judging a new idea as fit or unfit? In a free society the collective sum of incremental ideas allowed to succeed or fail on their own merits guides civilution with great flexibility and responsiveness. It is not surprising that the periods before the Renaissance, when kings and lords and clergy gave new ideas a very limited market, were called the Middle Ages and the Dark Ages. It is not a chance coincidence that the acceleration of science and prosperity in the western world followed the acceleration of freedom that began during the Renaissance.

If an innovative idea is an accident occurring from the combination of knowledge and attitudes, skills and habits of individual men, then the free market is the oxygen that fans the "emberonic" idea into an advance of civilization. The market enables a free citizenry to assign a price or value to each idea, causing it to be successfully developed or discarded according to that value. Through trial and error, success and failure new and valuable innovations are put into practice and become the foundation for the next generation of innovation. Since civilization is the sum of all the culture, ideas, innovations, ethics, organization and physical assets of a people, "civilution", this market driven free and organic growth process is how our civilization has come to grow so rapidly and prosper beyond the imagination of those who preceded us.

With this understanding of "civilution" the relationship of our liberty to our innovation and wealth becomes blindingly clear. Free exchange of ideas and freedom to experiment fertilize the environment for accidental collisions and combinations of knowledge birthing innovative ideas. Free markets allow free citizens to value those ideas and thereby decide which make good investments and which will be discarded. Limitations on exchange of ideas, on experimentation and on free markets, whatever their presumed merits; have the effect of retarding the development of civilization and reducing the wealth available to all citizens. To believe "progress" can be planned or predicted or even guided by kings or presidents or bureaucrats is to be supremely arrogant. It fails to credit the collective wisdom of all citizens and falsely presumes superior wisdom of the few who would assign themselves the power to plan, predict and guide.

Climate Change

There is only a small minority who admit to not knowing what causes climate change or what can or should be done about it. This minority has the advantage of skepticism when reading the latest pundits quoted in the daily press.

In 2013 a popular quote was, "The year 2012 was the warmest in history in North America, a full degree warmer than the record set in 1998." A quick Google search yields a different result for world temperatures, down in 2012, the second coolest year since 2000. This tidbit escaped the notice of those promoting carbon emissions as the root of disaster.

Also in 2013, frequently heard on the airways was "We are experiencing a terrible increase in natural disasters such as Hurricane Sandy, a once in a generation storm striking New York and New Jersey." How does a "once in a generation storm" lead to a conclusion of radical or even worrisome long-term change rather than a statistical accident?

These anecdotes prove nothing except that the dialog on global warming includes a great deal of hype and emotion.

There are currently 39 molecules of Carbon dioxide per 100,000 molecules in our atmosphere. This concentration is growing at a rate that will double in the twenty first century. Carbon dioxide in the atmosphere traps infrared radiation from the sun and in doing so tends to raise the temperature at the earth's surface. What is known for certain is that "scientific" models are all based on assumptions and have been consistently incorrect in predicting actual global temperature change. It is also known that there has been no recorded global wide warming in the first decade of the twenty first century. What is not known is what else in addition to carbon dioxide is causing or inhibiting climate change, whether it is cyclical or secular or what other natural forces may amplify or counterbalance the makeup of the atmosphere.

So what are we to think or do about global warming? Should we join the cacophony, assume that greenhouse gasses are the only problem and prepare for impending doom? Alternatively should we assume the whole issue is political baloney and hope for the best?

When seeking validation for a truth we think we already know, a different truth is seldom found. To find the whole truth one must seek a contradiction of that which is believed. Imagine a federal bureaucrat funding research on natural causes of climate change that might contradict dire establishment assumptions about the carbon footprint. Can we wonder why there is little funding for such research? Why did the Northwest Passage open up in 1939 and 1940 and then re-freeze as Arctic ice expanded? What is the compensating impact of increased evaporation in a warming world creating increased cloud cover and reflecting solar heat? What is the impact of cyclical changes in sun spot activity that peaked coincidentally with a peak of global temperatures in 1998? Since the sun causes all global warming, shouldn't our agenda include understanding cyclical changes in solar activity? Are we in denial of profound geological and meteorological evidence of radical natural climate shifts and cycles over the millennia?

Perhaps we should pay more attention to the several possibilities for the twenty first century. Surely any desirable possibility will include increasing wealth and energy consumption for nearly all the peoples of the world. Americans should applaud and welcome the great climb from poverty for billions in Asia and Africa. Even if we do not welcome it, we can do nothing to slow it.

With or without action by governments, as global wealth grows carbon based fuels will continue to become more scarce and more expensive, causing greater innovation and development of alternative energy sources. This may ultimately reduce our global carbon footprint, but for the first half of this century at least, it can at best serve only to slow its growth. All the efforts we might make cannot offset the growing demand from those who aspire to our standard of living. America cannot reduce fuel consumption enough in 15 to 20 million new cars per year to offset a billion bicycles and pedestrians being replaced by even the most efficient vehicles in Asia. If China and India alone increase their electric power consumption to United States per capita levels they will need to add more than five times the current power generating capacity of the United States. Most of that currently being planned or built will be powered by fossil fuels.

Knowing these things, we can predict with near certainty that the carbon in our atmosphere will more than double to over 80 molecules per 100,000 in this century, and that none of this growth will be generated in North America. What we do not know is what other compensating or multiplying or cyclical forces of nature will work in concert with this to change global temperature or climate. This is the most important question for researchers. Yet it is politically incorrect to ask anything that might dampen our panic or broaden our focus from avoiding inevitable oblivion. With such research we may discover that our global eco-system has its own healing mechanisms, or we may discover it can be horribly destabilized. In either case, we would be wise to be deliberate in our efforts both to moderate our carbon footprint and to prepare for results from the path we are already traveling. We are told that all scientists agree on these things, but they do not. We should never conclude that the volume of noise proves truth, but rather seek out the lonely voices that may add to our learning.

In the fourth century BC, Greek thinkers wrote that the earth and every planet revolved on its axis. Nearly two thousand years later, Europeans ridiculed Columbus for thinking the world was round. Forty years after Columbus, Copernicus' book, *On the Revolutions of the Celestial Spheres* was initially ridiculed. Most scientists and intellectuals held on to early assumptions contradicting the structure of our planetary system even though much contrary evidence had been observed and recorded. In retrospect Copernicus' book was a seminal event of the scientific revolution that followed. Perhaps we should open our minds to the reality that the nature and behavior of natural forces in our atmospheric ecosystem are at least as complex and mysterious today as were the movements of planets in Copernicus' time. To make dire worst case predictions about man's impact and to blindly bet that nature's response will be impotent is to risk impoverishing ourselves by trying to solve problems that do not exist or cannot be solved. It also risks not finding the best solutions for real threats not yet recognized.

Competition

Competition by its nature helps us to perfect ourselves, and makes us more unequal. We celebrate the athlete who hones skills and the coach who hones athletes and teams to record breaking championships.

We celebrate when our children run in races, and especially when they win. We cheer for our children and our schools and their teams to win, to be better than all the others in the race or in the game.

We celebrate the Olympic champion. He or she gets the gold medal, a plethora of lucrative sponsorships and opportunity for a lifetime of celebrity. We buy Wheaties with champions on the box. We buy shoes the champion wears. We hire the champion as coach for the next generation of champions.

It seems normal and appropriate that the fourth best in the world gets no medal, no sponsorships, no celebrity, only the thrill of competing with the best and the prospect for coaching some in the next generation. This inequality is necessary. If all entrants received the same prize, all would be less motivated for excellence!

We celebrate the champion quarterback, and we celebrate his $200 million contract. Yet we see as extravagant a similar package for a CEO who coaches and quarterbacks a multibillion dollar corporation, serving millions of customers who voluntarily spend their own money on its products and services, providing jobs and growth opportunities for tens of thousands of workers and contractors, providing security and returns on the investment of retirement funds and insurance reserves.

Should we celebrate Steve Jobs for revolutionizing smart phones? Should we celebrate Mark Zuckerberg for creating a whole new environment for social media used by over a billion people? Should we celebrate Sam Walton for revolutionizing retail logistics and Jeff Bezos for a new paradigm in on-line shopping or Jamie Dimon for a healthy J. P. Morgan Chase able to be part of the rescue of other banks in the 2008 financial collapse?

If these are champions, winning the competition in each of their fields, who is to judge whether the size of their prize is just or excessive or insufficient? It is a step on a very slippery slope to even ask the question. We live in a civilization built by free markets and free exchange. We have a constitution that protects the rights of property owners against search and seizure and expropriation. We have an economic and legal system based on the freedom of individuals. We cast all that aside if we override the judgment of buyers and sellers for the sake of "equity," or "equality" or "fairness." If some cannot win, then none will be best. If we demonize winners there will be fewer of them and we are all less well off. If we rig the game, who will be in charge of the rigging? Whoever it is will be in charge of us all.

Consumerism

It has been said that consumerism is an abundance of demand where there is no need. Surely contemporary American culture fits that description. One only needs to shop on Fifth Avenue or Worth Avenue or at Wal-Mart on Black Friday to validate this observation.

Some conclude that this is quite normal. Most of us want more than we have. Advertisers and sellers naturally try to create demand regardless of need.

Yet there is a huge risk to depending on things we do not need or acting on our desire for things we cannot afford. Gluttony, the second deadly sin is not a sin of the merchant. It is a sin of the consumer. It is cleansing to meditate from time to time on how little we really need and how a mountain of stuff often weighs down our lives. Would we be better off with more things and less understanding, or with fewer things and greater understanding?

Corruption

Corruption has one principal enabler. That enabler is the real or perceived power to spend other peoples' money or regulate the details of their lives and escape consequences.

There cannot be corruption when a well-informed buyer, of his own free will, makes a purchase with his own funds from a seller who faces competition!

Those in government are always spending someone else's (the taxpayer's) money. More and more, they now regulate and micromanage our lives. When the government or other monopolist weakens or interferes with free market transactions, the possibility and probability of corruption is introduced if not guaranteed.

This is the moral imperative for free markets and for limiting the scope of government. It is no accident that corruption is the greatest in industries and activities with the greatest government involvement and regulation. If this does not seem obvious, compare and contrast reports of corruption in immigration, public contracting, mortgage banking and Medicare to those in less regulated fields such as retail trade, printing, fashion design and semiconductors.

Curiosity

The child in all of us who asks why and how has a great advantage in life. First, it is much more difficult to fool the curious. The curious do not easily take anything as given. The curious want to understand the basis for any assertion, and thereby confound both the prevaricator and the naïve.

Plato's assertion that "Necessity is the mother of invention." misses the mark. Necessity may be the midwife of invention, but curiosity is its mother.

There is seldom an entirely new idea. Every "new" idea is an accidental intersection of old ideas in a new context. The curious individual accumulates a better understanding of a more diverse collection of ideas, simply because of the many hows and whys asked over a lifetime. The curious are thus better prepared to find the intersection of seemingly unrelated ideas with whatever problem is at hand. Curiosity provides the best possible seedbed for innovation.

Debt

Accumulating debt is like bleeding to death. A need is perceived, and resources are spent before they are on hand. At the moment, it feels as innocent as a pinprick. It feels so much better to enjoy the consumption than to avoid the pinprick. Surely we can manage a bit of debt. But we cannot put the blood back into the vein, and enjoying today with the promise to pay tomorrow becomes a cascading addiction.

Bleeding to death is not painful. Even at the point of no return, the organism feels fatigue, perhaps some euphoria of relaxation, but not pain. The last realization, that it is no longer possible to control one's own destiny, comes gradually. So it is with debt. There comes a moment when our destiny is controlled by our creditors. We are no longer in charge of our lives! The moment may seem a surprise, but it cannot be so to a perceptive observer.

This inevitable moment comes with equal devastation to individuals, households, businesses and governments. Eventually all debt must be paid or repudiated. The moment of bankruptcy is the moment the borrower is no longer in charge.

The antidote for debt is a financial plan and the discipline to follow it. The destiny of a household without a plan or budget is debt. The household with a budget allocates its resources to achieve its needs and priorities. The budget brings into focus the reality that more of one thing means less of another. More vacation means less for tuition. A bigger house means a smaller car. Everything is a choice.

The same is true for a business. Every part of a business organization has its resources and responsibilities. If sales cannot meet its goals within its planned expenditures, an alarm goes off as the business is threatened. The same is true for manufacturing or research or accounting or any aspect of the business. The budget is a tool for setting priorities and making choices. Without such a tool, there are always things that "must" be done after all the resources have been spent, hence debt.

The same is true for government. The need for schools, roads, streetcars, police, firemen and other government services must all be weighed against each other in light of available revenues. At least that is true for local and state governments who are limited in their ability to issue debt and print money.

National governments, ours in particular, play by a different set of rules. Even if a budget is in place, there is no incentive or necessity to use it as a tool. New programs have "estimated costs", but once in place, no one is accountable for managing to those costs. Congress can attach unplanned expenditures to any bill. Bureaucrats can rewrite rules and benefits with accountability to no one. Our culture of government subsidies is anathema to any discipline of weighing priorities. How does one weigh the merits of a few million dollars for streetcars in New Orleans vs. community organizers in Chicago vs. urban parks in New Jersey vs. all the other possible uses for grants, earmarks, entitlements, regulations and staff additions made each year? Stop for a moment and ask, "How could the wisest possible government in Washington sensibly manage the diverse, distant and unrelated priorities across every neighborhood and family in this great nation? We are doomed to unmanageable debt because we try to centralize local responsibilities.

Most corporations and families have at one time or another faced a financial crisis. Plans and budgets have not been working.

Debt has been accumulating. The unexpected has occurred. The current path is unsustainable. These crises are moments for making choices. We re-assess, put all our goals and expenditures on the table and restructure our lives with a new sustainable plan, or we fail. Families and businesses tighten their belts, reduce waste and defer some priorities. These are healthy exercises. They force us to improve our productivity, to rethink our assumptions and values and once resolved we move on with more energy and less stress.

Governments, especially national governments tend to see all expenditures as necessary. They tend not to reassess priorities, rather to raise taxes and borrow or print money, all of which impoverish their citizens. Just as for families and businesses, failure to restructure to a realistic plan ultimately leads to bankruptcy for nations. Collecting more taxes and printing more money can delay but not avoid the inevitability. John Adams understood this when he wisely observed, "There are two ways to conquer and enslave a nation. One is by the sword, the other is by debt."

I owe credit for much wisdom to my father who published the following epigram, commenting on our government's fiscal discipline, over sixty years ago:

FANTASY

In the wondrous land of Make Believe
Next door to Tisn't So
All the men are little boys
And money bushes grow.

The ladies all have pretty clothes
And servants by the score.
They never want for anything-

Just charge it at the store.

A mystic Uncle runs the place,
Though he is never seen.
He's said to have a silly book
Called *Equity and Lien.*

This book is bigger than his house
And higher than his head,
With neither words nor pictures–
Just numbers, all bright red.

He has more wealth than you can think,
Just piles of I.O.U.s.
And every day he signs some more
To pay those coming due.

I bet you couldn't be that smart,
Not even if you tried.
I wonder what would 'come of us
If Uncle ever died?

Democracy

We often think of democracy as beginning with the Magna Carta, but it is a much older idea. Plato described, "Democracy, which is a charming form of government, full of variety and disorder, and dispensing a sort of equality to equals and unequals alike."

Plato and Aristotle both thought democracy was fragile and inevitably passes into despotism. Plato described spendthrifts as the ruin of Democracy. His ideas and his language in *The Republic* are eerily contemporary today!

"I refer to the class of spendthrifts, of whom the more courageous are the leaders and the more timid the followers. We compare them to drones, some stingless, and others having stings…. Freedom creates more drones in the democracy… In the oligarchical state they are disqualified and driven from office…. Whereas in a democracy they are almost the entire ruling power, and while the keener sort speak and act, the others keep buzzing about the bema and do not suffer a word to be said on the other side, hence in a democracy almost everything is managed by the drones." (spendthrifts)….

"There is another class…. The orderly class, which in a nation of traders is sure to be the richest. They are the most squeezable persons and yield the largest amount of honey to the drones…

"The people are the third class consisting of those who work with their hands; they are not politicians and have not much to live upon… This, when assembled is the largest and most powerful class in a democracy… but then the multitude is seldom willing to congregate unless they get a little honey… and the end is that they see the people, not of their own accord but through ignorance and because they are deceived... they do not wish to be, but the sting of the drones torments them and breeds revolution in them...

"The people always have some champion whom they set over and nurse to greatness. This and no other, is the root from which a tyrant springs; when he first appears above ground he is a protector.

"How, then does the protector begin to change into a tyrant?

"In the tale of the Arcadian temple of Lycaean Zeus, he who has tasted the entrails of a single human victim minced up with the entrails of other victims is destined to become a wolf...

"And the protector of the people is like him; having a mob at his disposal, he is not restrained from shedding the blood of kinsmen.... Must he not perish at the hands of his enemies, or from being a man become a wolf – that is a tyrant? Inevitably."

Many of our founders, particularly the Federalists, had read Plato, and tried to protect us against the failures he predicted. It is daunting that his warning from 21 centuries before the founding of our great republic predicted the inevitability of overtaxing, overspending, political correctness, attacks on the "one percent" and the impoverishment of the middle class. It is worthy of our attention to ponder how we prevent his final prediction, our passing into despotism.

Disparity

Increasingly we see headlines and articles about the record levels of disparity between the wealthy and the poor, or the "one percent" and the middle class. We read that the income of the wealthiest few has grown 75 times faster than that of the less fortunate. We hear that the fabric of our society is threatened by this unfair result of capitalism and greed.

There is nothing new about condemning disparity and greed. Theodore Roosevelt, the "Trust Busting" President was an early advocate of populism. Roosevelt was born in 1858 with a long pedigree of wealth and privilege. He served as President of the United States from 1901 through 1908 with concentration and corruption of wealth as major themes of his administration. He referred to the "Robber Barron's" as "Malefactors of great wealth." The wealthiest men during his lifetime were John D. Rockefeller, Cornelius Vanderbilt and Andrew Carnegie. The combined wealth of these three men was just over 3.65 percent of our nation's Gross National Product. They are still three of the four wealthiest men in the history of America.

While the wealthy of the time built mansions on Fifth Avenue, Prairie Avenue, East Hampton and Lake Geneva, most of the country did not fare so well. The high school graduation rate across the nation was less than 10 percent. There were few automobiles, no home refrigerators or washing machines. Fewer than half the population had indoor plumbing. The average urban apartment contained only a few hundred square feet and included no running water. Nascent labor unions were only beginning to impact industrial wages. Thirty one percent of our population lived on farms. The average farm was 138 acres and supported five people. Farmers tilled with power from horses, mules or oxen.

Few had either electricity or running water. At that time there was no income tax or social security benefits. There were no farm support prices, no food stamps or welfare or unemployment benefits or housing or medical subsidies.

It is difficult to imagine and impossible to prove that disparity of living conditions between the least and most wealthy in America today is even close to that at the turn of the last century. Would it not be frustrating and hopeless to believe that all our economic growth and all our efforts for over a century to accomplish greater "economic justice" have resulted in nothing?

The most frequently quoted statistics about contemporary income disparity come directly from Census data tables. Nineteen eighty was the most recent year when the "99 percent" earned 90 percent of U.S. national income. In the period between 1980 and 2012 the purchasing power of income of the bottom 20 percent of U.S. households rose by 0.5 percent. Not 0.5 percent annually, 0.5 percent over a 32-year period. The next 20 percent of households improved their purchasing power by 4.3 percent while the top five percent improved theirs by 72.5 percent.

Before we conclude the real causes and dangers of growth of disparity between rich and poor, we should realize four truths about this data.

First, the frequently quoted numbers are not complete. The data do not include federal transfer payments biased heavily toward the poor. Medicaid, nutrition subsidies, public assistance, unemployment payments and Social Security total 1.5 trillion dollars or 10 percent of national income and are for the most part not included in data describing the share of income consumed by the "99 percent".

Second, the data are adjusted for inflation and the consumer price index. The unadjusted Census numbers show much less growth in disparity. In current year dollars, the lowest 20 percent gained 3.1 percent annually while the top 5 percent gained 4.9 percent annually. Adjusting the numbers is at best an imperfect science. At worst it is biased to make a political point.

Why do we need to adjust the data? Government policy to expand the money supply and pay debt with cheaper dollars causes the inflation we adjust for. To the extent we fund our government with borrowed money, we ultimately create inflation and thereby impose the cost on those who can least afford it.

Third, the "one percent" is an exceptionally fluid group. It includes CEOs of many public and private corporations and many non-profits. It includes university presidents and some professors, the President of the United States and most senators, many of your favorite musicians, movie producers and stars and best selling authors. It includes every athlete on the roster of an NHL, NFL, NBA or Major League Baseball team and all their head coaches. It includes many doctors and lawyers. Most people do not spend their entire life in this group. Most are in this group because other people believe they contribute value commensurate with their income, and if that perceived value does not continue they will fall out of the group as quickly as they entered.

Similarly, people in 2012 are not the same as the people in 1980 statistics. There were 82,368 households in the United States in 1980. With an adult life cycle of around 60 years, only about 40,000 of these households still exist. In 2012 we had 122,459 households, of which only about one third existed in 1980. The older households, headed by individuals with 30 years more experience surely have gained in share of income through labor, learning, saving and investing. Very few have stood still and let younger generations pass them by. The great majority of those with the lowest incomes are younger, less experienced and with less capital. What the data do show is that those who reach the top 60 percent of incomes get a larger reward today than did their fathers and mothers. It does seem as difficult as ever for the lower 40 percent to get started only if you ignore a one trillion dollar increase in transfer payments since 1980, mostly to this group. Perhaps we should ignore these added subsidies. Even though they are additions to income they create dependency, not wealth or investment. This leads to a final point:

The most important disparity issue in our civilization is the preservation of disparate possibilities, that is the opportunity for upward mobility. John D. Rockefeller's father was a traveling salesman, leaving the family for extended periods. Young John worked to help support his mother, was graduated from high school in Cleveland, Ohio where he also took a ten-week course in accounting. His first job paid 50 cents per day. Cornelius Vanderbilt's father operated a ferry in New York Harbor. Young Cornelius quit school at age eleven to work on his father's ferry and started his own ferry business at age sixteen. Andrew Carnegie was born in Dunfermline, Scotland in a weaver's cottage his family shared with another weaver's family. In 1848 his father fled from famine for a better life in America. At age thirteen, to help pay the families debts, Carnegie took a job as a bobbin boy in a cotton factory in Pittsburg. His starting wage was $1.20 for a 72-hour week. Henry Ford's father migrated from Ireland to a farm in Michigan. Ford left home at age sixteen to work as an apprentice machinist in Detroit, Michigan. These men produced the four greatest fortunes in American History, and enabled countless other fortunes for suppliers, distributors, agents, employees and customers. Each gave substantial amounts from their fortunes to found hospitals, universities and charitable foundations. These are only four of thousands of stories of entrepreneurs in America who came and still come from obscurity. With imagination and hard work they create millions of opportunities for others both through their enterprise and through philanthropy. The environment that encourages such enterprise, lets it thrive and succeed or fail on its own merits is truly the goose that lays golden eggs for us all.

Economics

There is a virtuous economic cycle available to every nation on earth, and the prosperity of the people in each nation is largely dependent on how that economic cycle is managed. Briefly stated, the cycle is:

- Human needs are perceived;
- Capital is invested to provide capacity to satisfy these needs;
- Labor is employed;
- Products and services are delivered;
- Proceeds from products and services return to providers of capital and labor;
- Proceeds are used to purchase other goods and services, to create new needs and new capital, thus renewing the virtuous cycle.

Economists find many things to disagree about, but nearly all agree on two realities. Most fundamental is the mechanism of a free market. In a free market, individual buyers and sellers balance supply and demand via millions of individual transactions that determine what is produced and what prices are paid. Adam Smith called this the invisible hand of the market. If more corn is produced than can be sold, the price of corn falls. When the price goes down, more consumers will buy corn instead of other foods and the least efficient corn farmers look for other crops they can grow at a higher profit. Through a multitude of individual decisions, a balance between supply and demand of every product and service is achieved at a price acceptable to both buyers and sellers. Every individual in the market votes with his or her wallet, and the collective judgment of these votes determines prices and rewards those who produce the greatest value. In the eyes of the market participants, the maximum possible wealth is created through this balance. When the balance is disrupted the result is surpluses and shortages and waste.

The second subject of agreement among economists is that government balance sheets are important and money like all else is subject to the law of supply and demand. Nations have the unique option to print money. When a government prints money in excess of its real wealth, the money becomes cheap and prices of everything money buys go up. Savings of the citizenry depreciate, and government pays back debt with cheaper dollars. Printing too much money and making it too easily available is the root cause of rising prices, inflation and asset bubbles.

Economists disagree about how to best manage these economic forces in an imperfect world. How do we protect the free market from predatory forces of deception and monopoly? How do we regulate economic growth to maintain prosperity and minimize the pain of boom and bust cycles? How do we provide incentives or requirements that will allocate resources more beneficially than an unregulated free market would accomplish?

Congress passed the first antitrust law, the Sherman Act, in 1890 as a "comprehensive charter of economic liberty aimed at preserving free and unfettered competition as the rule of trade." Since that time many laws and regulations have been enacted to regulate mergers, agreements and relationships among competitors, disclosure of product information and discriminatory pricing. Some economists see current regulations and regulatory agencies as too meddlesome and too extensive but nearly all agree that government has an important role in the preservation of competitive markets.

Adam Smith laid the foundation of modern economics in his *An Inquiry into the Nature and causes of the Wealth of Nations*, published in 1776. He described the "invisible hand" of the competitive market creating the maximum wealth through the actions of each player acting in his own self-interest. He also predicted increasing division of labor and advocated the laissez faire economic policies that characterized most of the nineteenth century. Smith's position as the most read and followed economic thinker lasted for 160 years until John Maynard Keynes published his *General Theory of Employment Interest and Money* in 1936. Keynes pioneered the idea that governments can and should manage economic growth and the business cycle through fiscal and monetary policy. Keynes wrote convincingly and had a revolutionary impact on economic thought and policy throughout the western world in the twentieth century. He also saw but could not alter the futility of implementing much of his own work.

Keynes was appointed financial representative for the British Treasury to the 1919 Versailles peace conference. He saw the resulting peace treaty as unworkable and dangerous. In his *The Economic Consequences of Peace* published in 1919 he foresaw the consequences leading to the catastrophe that followed in Europe. He wrote, "Moved by insane delusion and reckless self regard, the German people overturned the foundations on which we all lived and built. But the spokesmen of the French and British peoples have run the risk of completing the ruin, which Germany began, by a peace which, if it is carried into effect, must impair yet further, when it might have restored, the delicate, complicated organization, already shaken and broken by war...."

Three years later, still railing against the Versailles treaty, he opened his 1922 book, *A Revision of Treaty*, with this statement: "It is the method of modern statesmen to talk as much folly as the public demand and to practice no more of it than is compatible with what they have said..."

So it has been since and still is today. Governments in their zeal to encourage prosperity over stimulate until economies overheat and then recreate the same problems through efforts to shorten or moderate the resulting down cycle. Some economists believe we have learned from our mistakes in past recessions. Others argue that we will also learn from the new mistakes we are making today.

Finally, the question of how we provide incentives or requirements that will allocate resources more beneficially is a question of politics, not economics. The free and unfettered market as the rule of trade unquestionably creates the greatest wealth for society. Every departure from the free market has a cost. The political question is, "Is the benefit of altering the free market outcome worth that cost?" Governments depart from the free market frequently to control prices or trade or to provide aid to the needy or to protect the environment or to invest in infrastructure. There is always a cost of not making different investments the free market might have dictated. That cost is seldom discussed.

When listening to politicians pontificate on these matters, it is useful to remember, and hold them accountable that each departure from the free market is a tradeoff, giving up wealth creation and freedom in exchange for a theoretical gain in safety or security or justice. It is also important to realize that giving power to regulators or bureaucracies is not necessarily giving it to wiser or more disinterested people than we find in the free marketplace. As with any purchase, the goals and costs of economic incentives and market distortions should be clear and measured. These are political choices, not imperatives, and they are not free.

Education

My grandparents began their education in one-room schoolhouses. The staple textbooks, McGuffey readers, taught phonics, vocabulary, classics and moral values. Teachers were educated, but there were no degrees in "Education." If children did not stay focused, parents were called in, and parents knew the importance of making their children accountable. Children brought their own lunches and played games they could make up in the schoolyard. There were no Coke or candy machines, no television or electronic games, no organized soccer or baseball and no excuses.

These children grew up, most without high school diplomas and very few with the benefit of a college education. They became the parents of the greatest generation. Their children saved the world from tyranny and created the most productive and most generous nation the world has ever known.

Today, one third of eighth grade students in U.S. public schools read at grade level proficiency. Thirty percent of eighth grade students in U.S. public schools understand mathematics at grade level with proficiency. One quarter drop out before finishing high school. Any private or parochial school performing at this "average" level would have no customers. Any home schooling family with this result would be deemed unfit to home school their children.

The U.S. Department of Education produced a *Strategy for Education Equity and Excellence* in 2010. The top three strategies recommended (in order) were equitable (more) school finance, raising pay for teachers, and early childhood education.

Contrary to the politically correct view, money is demonstrably not the problem with education in the United States. The two states with the least expenditure per student (Utah and Idaho) spent 65 percent less than the two with greatest expenditure (New York and Washington, DC) yet their students outperform in reading and math skills and high school graduation rates.

The average annual starting salary for college graduates in the humanities and social science in 2009 was $37,000, precisely equal to the national average starting teacher salary. The report's recommended forty-eight percent salary increase nationwide will do nothing to improve existing teachers. It disregards the reality that many private and parochial school teachers work for less than public school scale for their own reasons and that Teach For America volunteers, some of the most effective "rookie" teachers, work for subsistence wages by choice. It ignores the need for teacher accountability for student performance.

The Head Start program has been in place for forty-seven years and along with other government-funded pre-schools currently serves forty-two percent of all four year olds in America. In 2012 the Health and Human Services Department reported a decade long study of Head Start. The key finding was, "Looking across the full study period, from the beginning of Head Start through third grade, the evidence is clear that access to Head Start improved children's preschool outcomes across developmental domains, but had few impacts on children in kindergarten through third grade." Early childhood education is important and can be effective, but federal efforts have been an unqualified failure.

Clearly the authors of this *Strategy for Education Equity and Excellence* document suffered from too much job security. The flaw in our national dialog is reflected in the title. We need to be less concerned with equity for the poor and the teachers and more focused on excellence for every individual teacher and student.

We need to stop blaming the poor and recognize that many public schools are not just failing the poor. They are failing all their students, all of our children. They are also failing the ten percent of K–12 students in private and parochial schools and their parents who feel they must pay twice for their children's education. Our government does not even have the courage to compare public school performance statistics to this group. When Equity becomes a surrogate word for Equality, it becomes the enemy of Excellence.

Professional sports have perhaps the highest observable concentration of hugely successful people who come from the humblest beginnings. The players have honed their skills to championship levels and most have made it through college. When the rookies first get on camera we most frequently hear, "Thanks Mom!"

Moms and dads, rich and poor know that kids will do what is expected and demanded of them. They know that without discipline, the brightest kids can be the most troublesome. They know that each child is an individual who has different assets, different limitations and learns differently. They also know that none of these differences can be an excuse for lowering standards or expectations or for a child doing less than his or her personal best. And they know that values are important. If parents do not know these things, or cannot learn them, there is no hope.

I have lived many years in Chicago and many years in New Orleans. In both of these cities, it is not news and no secret that Catholic schools outperform most public schools by almost any measure, and they do so at a much lower cost. Perhaps it is because they are not very modern. They teach the basics first. They demand discipline and hold parents accountable. The schools are run for the children, not for the teachers. They teach values as well as knowledge. Because of all these things, they get great support and re-enforcement from their community. Parents pay to send their children even though they have already paid taxes for "free" public education. This is not just true in Chicago and New Orleans, but these cities offer exceptionally visible demonstrations.

The Federal Department of Education spends about 70 billion dollars annually or a little over 1,000 dollars for every child in the United States from two to eighteen years old. Very little of this money is being used in the front lines of education. According to its own strategy statement it advocates much more money, no more accountability and little acknowledgement of the wisdom of the citizenry. If we sent those dollars back to the states or municipalities or even better, to the moms and dads, it could surely be spent more directly and more effectively on education for their children.

What would happen if we gave the power of school boards to the parents and citizens of each individual school, and gave each principal the responsibility and authority of any manager? That is, to manage the school including curricula, materials, staff, schedules, etc. to accomplish education goals set with the board (parents).

This is the model that educated my grandparents. Charter schools are not the only approach, but this is the model of many Charter Schools. It is beginning to work dramatically in many communities. We hear many arguments against this radical approach, to empower those who can be held accountable, but none of these arguments focus on the needs of students or the competence of parents.

Parents are not too dumb or too busy to lead. Good teachers will have more security without unions in a decentralized system than with them in centralized bureaucracies. Students can hardly become worse off.

Why don't we commit our faith and our future to the parents, give them back the schools and tell them that they are in charge. Give the people or local governments back the "Education" money they now send to Washington and let them be accountable. Clearly this cannot be accomplished in one day, or perhaps it can. It can never be accomplished if we do not aggressively move in a new direction.

Michael Moffitt

Education, Post Secondary

Too often we hear the question, "Is college worth what it costs?" We cannot afford for that to be the central question. The right question is, "What is our vision for effective and affordable post secondary education?"

The crisis in college costs is in part a re-run of the home mortgage crisis. Washington has decided that everyone needs to go to college, whether they can afford it or not, whether they are qualified or not or whether college education provides a valuable basis for their life plan or not. We create demand by providing subsidies and "easy" credit, not reminding the borrowers that no debt is "easy" to repay. As we learned (or should have learned) in freshman Economics, creating more demand causes prices to rise.

We have created even more demand by encouraging colleges and universities to admit less than fully qualified candidates. Many colleges and universities have remedial courses for those "not ready for the core curriculum." Surely these cost a great deal more on a college campus than they would at a high school or community college or on the Internet. With the availability of these resources, we should be raising the bar for university entrance, not lowering it.

One might think that the Internet should be a huge part of our vision. Yet student loan and default data suggest that "Internet Universities" are still expensive and their graduates are not in great demand in the marketplace. These are a part of the government funding bubble as well. Why, one might ask, shouldn't internet courses be exceptionally inexpensive? Presentations of the highest quality can be re-used many times. There is no requirement for bricks and mortar, for dormitories or student unions or for food service or athletics. Many of our finest universities offer free courses over the internet, some exact replicas of classroom courses including individual communications among the students and with the professor.

So, here is Granddad's vision for college education for his grandchildren. First, no university worthy of the name will accept them for on campus work unless they are fully qualified. All remedial courses and all freshman and sophomore level curriculum will be available on line. Financial aid to students who have not fulfilled requirements available on line will be limited to a subsidized computer and a discount on already very inexpensive on line tuition. Entrance to on campus courses for more advanced work will be conditional on achievement in the on-line environment.

My grandchildren might complain about the loss of all the wonderful campus life that their parents and I enjoyed, and the ruination of college athletics, and all the social learning from our experience away from home. I hope they are wise enough not to be surprised by my lack of sympathy and my questions; "Are you going to college to develop your mind and better prepare yourself to be a valuable member of society? How does "campus life" in your first two years contribute to that goal?" Should "campus life" be financed by others or required for all, or should there be a choice with accountability. I hope they will also recognize the opportunity to begin college work on line before they have completed high school.

This vision could create capacity to double the number of college graduates without adding any more on campus investment. The technology is available and being used today. Quality course materials are emerging at an accelerating pace. Increasing the capacity (supply) will force prices to fall. It is my belief and hope that this vision will come to pass, sooner rather than later if markets are allowed to operate and government stands aside and lets it happen.

In this process a new balance will be achieved. Strong universities will become stronger, will have more scholarship money for upperclassmen, will upgrade the quality of their offerings and will attract more students. Less productive campuses will close or be repurposed to vocational skill training. Internet only universities will lack the intellectual capital to compete in "academia" but will compete with community colleges for skills training. Undergraduate degrees will have more and higher quality content, thus raising the bar for graduate programs. Universities will perhaps even return toward their historic focus of "Universal" education of the whole student, allowing those primarily seeking instruction to find it in a less demanding, less expensive environment.

All this is possible with existing technology and will happen without any bureaucratic intervention or subsidy. Through this vision our children will all be able to have more accessible and better education than their parents and grandparents and the rest of the world. It can happen very quickly if we stop subsidizing last century's model.

Elegance

To describe one as elegant is perhaps the supreme compliment. Elegance is richness and effectiveness with or through simplicity and balance. The elegant woman is trim and fit, dressed in simple but well designed fashion, erect and alert. Elegance is depreciated by slouch, fat, gaudiness or complication.

The most elegant innovations are also the most powerful and enriching. The wheel, movable type, the transistor; each set history on an entirely new path. The paper clip, the coat hanger, the snap top can; each is simple and useful; each captures a small but secure niche in millions of lives. How many of the thousands of patents processed every year can make either claim.

We could learn a great deal about our institutions by applying elegance as a standard. Our tax code, writhes in complexity and seeks to achieve too many goals. Definitely not elegant. Our approach to management of financial markets, responding to every crisis with a new overlay of regulation, never peeling back the regulations or regulators who failed to predict or prevent the last crisis. Hardly elegant! In our legal system, the cost of securing justice is frequently disproportionate to the injustice. In our legislative process we create laws with thousands of pages that generate tens of thousands of rules and procedures and millions of dollars in bureaucratic payrolls. No elegance here!

In this world of great complexity, we should strive where possible to return to the elegance of our ancestors' character and commitment as expressed in the most elegant statements in history, the Ten Commandments, the Golden Rule, the Magna Carta, the Declaration of Independence and the United States Constitution.

Michael Moffitt

Equality

Nowhere in the wisdom of the ages is it said that we are all equally smart, equally talented, equally righteous, equally deserving or equally lucky. Nowhere is it written that we should be equally rich, equally healthy, or equally revered. Nowhere has there ever existed a civilization without huge discrepancies in power, wealth and intelligence.

So what is meant when it is said, "All men are created equal?"

We are equal in our humanity. We are equally entitled to the symmetry of the golden rule. We are equally alone and equally subordinate to nature. We are equal under the Law. In all other respects it is clear that all men and women are not equal, and it is not possible they will become so.

To concentrate on achievement of equality of results, especially economic results, we must continuously take from those with more and give to those with less. Since we are not all equal in building wealth, this process of taking and giving will never achieve equality and thus it will only end when we destroy the incentive to produce more. It takes great care to assure that investments in and measurement of greater opportunity stay focused on opportunity and not on equal results. For the only time we ever become equal by all measures, is when we all become slaves.

Then of course, we will not be equal to those who made us equal, for they will be the masters.

Feminism

Bertha Rosanna Fenner was born on February 26, 1872, the daughter of pioneer Iowa farmers. She was the second child of Bradford Clark Fenner whose parents had traveled west from New York State and his wife Rhoda Underwood, an Iowa neighbor and widow with a young daughter. As a young woman Bertha moved from Iowa to Chicago. She was part of the great migration to the Columbian Exposition and opportunities it presented to make a new life. On May 16, 1897 she married Anson Meanor, a dashing and successful lawyer and judge in Chicago. Bertha and Anson had two children before he forsook her and his career for alcohol. They were divorced in 1912 and he died in 1917.

Bertha, far from family and home reached into herself and her community for strength. She sold encyclopedias ran book fairs at elementary schools, kept her family together, sent her children to college and saved enough to move to Palo Alto, California where she died in 1945. She could not vote for much of her adult life, but she found and made opportunities to take her from a 120-acre farm to independence and urban sophistication in Hyde Park and Palo Alto. She was not wealthy, but she was strong and her life was fruitful and eclectic. She raised and was loved by two children. Had she been a man she might have been described as an adventurer, a professional and an entrepreneur.

Bertha's second child was a daughter, Marion. Marion was born in Chicago on August 13, 1900. She attended The University of Chicago from pre-school in the Lab School through college. During college she worked summers at a "farmerette farm", raising food for the war effort and the nation. After graduation, Marion forged a career in advertising. Her employer and mentor was Morris Needham, an advertising pioneer and owner of the firm that bore his name. Marion was his "affirmative action" project because it was in his self-interest. She produced for him and for his clients. In 1932, Marion was unusually successful, a media buyer, coordinating client efforts at Chicago's World Fair, when she met an air conditioning contractor by the name of Roy Moffitt. Marion and Roy were married on October 22, 1934. At thirty-four years of age Marion threw off the success of her career for what she viewed as a more noble and fulfilling life's work. For the next twenty-two years she was dedicated to her home and raising three children. She gave them the values she had been given: curiosity, kindness, confidence and self-reliance. I was the youngest of her children.

Marion and Roy's marriage became unsatisfactory. It was not desperate, there was economic security, there was no physical violence or infidelity, but the spark and the respect had eroded over the years. At age fifty-six she made a decision to start over. She did not choose an easy path. She had modest finances, no recent marketable experience and a short career expectation. She started at the bottom, finding employment as a clerk, receptionist, office manager, sorority housemother and companion. There is no question that her age and lack of recent experience made her life difficult. Nor is there any doubt that she was, with great grace and fortitude, able to create a new and full life for herself. Could more be said of any person, man or woman who, for whatever reason, had to start over at the age of fifty-six?

At twenty-seven years old Ann Kirkeeide was a successful fashion buyer and retail store manager. She worked hard, was powerful and respected and, when we met had a greater income than I. She made an awesome transformation to her new career as my wife, mother of our children and activist in each of our communities. Like my mother, she gave her children values of curiosity, kindness and self-reliance. She was obsessed with building their self-confidence. She raised money for schools, zoos and museums. She fought for neighborhood, environmental and safety issues. Her homes were always welcoming and stylish. She was as totally dedicated to her chosen career as a wife and mother as she had been to fashion merchandising.

Ann died at age sixty-four after living only eight years in her adopted home of New Orleans. It says a good deal about her impact that nearly two hundred people attended her memorial service. I'm sure if it had been my memorial after a successful thirty-eight-year career in business, many fewer would have bothered to come.

As I think about these three women who have shaped my life, it is hard to think of them as oppressed in any way. Each of them from time to time surely felt the sting of male chauvinism, but they did not allow that sting to limit their personal fulfillment. Clearly there is discrimination and unfairness, and there are great heroines who have fought for opportunities for women. But those who focus only on the unfairness miss an important part of the message. There have always been heroines. Women from Joan of Arc to Susan B. Anthony to Mother Theresa have profoundly affected history. First ladies like Abigail and Mary Todd and Eleanor and Hillary were powerful women behind and because of their husband's power, or perhaps it was the other way around? How many women like Bertha and Marion and Ann have crafted successful lives on their own terms? What limits any woman from doing the same?

In 1934 Marion wrote in her journal, "The woman who expects to succeed is seldom beaten; the woman who believes in her work finds that her faith is justified; the woman who is happy in her work finds that it is illuminated by her joy." When individual women believe as Marion did, and act on their belief, it becomes true. If instead they focus on perceptions of limits and injustice those become real as well.

Sarah Moffitt Pike was born on October 8, 1975, the third child of Ann and Michael. Sarah is of the generation writing a triumphant chapter on feminism. She is able to manage home and family and career on her own terms, enabled both by technology and communications and by political and social change. Ask these four generations of women, each in their time, "What is most important, most demanding and rewarding in your life?" The instant and unequivocal answer; "Our children!"

Forgiveness

Forgiveness is something we do for ourselves. The motivation for forgiving is not generosity or godliness. Forgiving others makes it possible to forgive ourselves. It relieves the stress of bitterness. It releases us from the grip of guilt and vengeance. In this light, we can better see the power of forgiving those who do not believe they need forgiveness. That is even more powerful and liberating than to offer forgiveness to one who pleads for it.

Forgiving does not mean forgetting or not learning. There is a huge difference between forgiveness and baseless trust. If forgiving means forgetting or not learning, then we can never forgive one we cannot trust, but that is not the case. We can wipe the slate clean, escape from our bitterness and offer our friendship even to one who has not earned our trust. We can forgive a man for killing our brother without laying ourselves down in front of his sword. In truth, failure to forgive would make it more likely that, in vengeance, we find ourselves facing that sword.

Goals

My father was insane about goals. When a young man called on my high school age sisters, he had to pass the gauntlet of my father's question, "What is your goal in life?" Being the youngest and only son, I faced that same gauntlet daily. Throughout my youth I mostly finessed the question, sharing only short and medium term goals.

Being an obedient son, I did strive to find an overarching goal for my life. My best effort was "to ride on "fast trains" that take me through life at a brisk and intensive pace and to leave every stopover a better place than I found." That satisfied me and has served me well, but I never sensed it would meet my father's standard, so I never shared it with him.

Throughout my life I have come to better understand my father's meaning. Mine was a goal to guide me wherever I found myself, but it was not a goal of where I would go. Most people who reach positions of great success or wealth or influence do not do so by accident. They are typically driven and focused on getting to their ultimate destination. They are frequently blessed by good fortune that helps them hit their goal. Yet luck is preparation meeting opportunity. Without the preparation, the opportunity is often invisible.

Every pilot, before he starts his engines, files a flight plan. He knows where he is going and by what route. His flight is coordinated with others by controllers to avoid mishaps. He knows the winds and his fuel requirements. He has performed his checklist. A pilot is taught that without a plan he is lost. Without a plan, one has no direction and cannot recognize the good luck of a tail wind or the bad luck of a head wind.

The right goal and plan is different for every individual. Some like to drift with the wind and enjoy the adventure. Some want to perfect themselves and set internal or family goals. Some want to change the world in a particular way or to strive to be the best at a particular endeavor. Some want to accumulate political power or wealth or fame. The lesson for every young person is to decide early in life what kind of goal and plan will lead toward your best life, to make your flight plan and follow it with dedication and vigor. Always remember that if you aim at a target and pull the bowstring strongly you might be lucky enough to hit a bull's eye. If you don't take careful aim, who knows where your arrow will fall?

Michael Moffitt

Greed

Greed is a lot like garlic. Used properly, garlic adds complexity and delicacy with a little kick. It stimulates our taste buds. It gives our diet variety and interest. Yet as a diet staple, garlic provides little nourishment and makes our every pore reek.

Like garlic, we love greed. We applaud "incentives" that appeal to the individual's greed to motivate doing the right thing. We love markets that provide natural profit incentives for productivity and for providing valuable products. Greed sharpens our wits. It stimulates creativity and risk, without which tomorrow would be just like yesterday. Yet if greed is our only motivator, it motivates only corruption.

We may believe a chef uses too much garlic because we like less intensity. We may pass on roasted garlic. We may be jealous of a chef's skill at spicing his stew. Yet most of us recognize a wide range of reasonable uses for garlic. It is usually not difficult to distinguish garlic as a spice from garlic as a dietary staple.

Similarly, we may believe some individuals are too successful, or others share too little. Even so, we should be careful not to confuse success with greed. There is no such thing as too much success when accompanied by integrity. Nor is there any meaningful success without integrity. But it is as hard to find any success without a dash of greed, as it is to find delicious cuisine with no spice.

Guns

The right to bear arms is protected in Article II of our Bill of Rights. This protection was not intended for hunters and hobbyists. The authors of our constitution intended to assure that every citizen has the right to defend self, home and family. They knew that, had they not had the ability to fight the kings' soldiers, there would be no constitution and no republic. They were also unwilling to put all their trust in any government in their time or at any future time.

All ten of the articles in the Bill of Rights limit the power of government. None were meant to protect us from criminals or from the insane or from ourselves. Each article has the sole purpose to protect the people from their government. It is no coincidence that the right to bear arms was protected in the second article, ahead of the right to be secure in our persons and homes, ahead of all judicial protections. The right to bear arms was placed ahead of all rights save freedom of religion, speech, the press, free assembly, and the right to petition government, all protected in the First Amendment. We should all hope that the courts continue to turn back all challenges to this right. If some of the constitution does not mean what it says, then who is to say any of it does.

How is it possible to regulate or abridge a constitutional right other than by constitutional amendment? Should citizens' rights be limited to having arms less effective than those easily available to any criminal? Should a citizen be as able to defend himself in the same way the police or militia are equipped to defend other citizens? Does the government have the right to take those rights away, or the responsibility to protect them? It is precisely the purpose of the second amendment to protect that right of self-defense. There is no ambiguity in the constitution or in court rulings on prior challenges.

Can we require licenses to operate a gun as we do automobiles? Driving an automobile is not a right protected by the constitution. We do not require licenses or permits to exercise free speech or freedom of religion, or to be secure in our homes. Freedom and individual rights are at times inconvenient and messy, but it is delusional to believe that evil people will not avail themselves of guns or whatever means necessary to violate the rights and lives of others. There are many things we can do to protect ourselves, yet we never get real protection by giving up the right to protect ourselves, or by disregarding the one document that protects all our rights.

Clearly we can prohibit convicted felons from owning weapons. That would not be cruel or unusual punishment. With appropriate due process we could also prohibit mentally ill individuals from gun ownership. If we have an easily accessible database of those prohibited individuals, we could prohibit sales of firearms to them. These things will help to keep guns out of dangerous hands, but not even a complete prohibition will keep guns out of the hands of those who would do evil with them. We learned that about alcohol. We are learning it about drugs. It would be foolhardy to believe any new or different lesson could come from gun prohibition.

Humility

Popular usage would have "humility" mean self-abasement or lack of pride. Pride is the first of the seven deadly sins, yet humility has little relationship to common usage of either pride or self-abasement.

One can be justifiably proud of human accomplishments or relationships. Deference can be as dangerous as pride if deference is toward a despot or a wrong or a mediocre standard.

Humility is a virtue as expressed in relation to the uniqueness of our existence. No creature other than Man can conceive and build a better world for himself. No other species can step outside of the moment or the self and be awed by our very existence. Only we can ask, "Where did I come from?" Or "How can I perfect myself?" Or "How can I improve the world around me?" That is the awesome gift we all share. That gift is the fundamental of our equality, as we all share it equally. Failure to be humble before that gift and toward all who have received it is truly the first deadly sin.

Michael Moffitt

Idealism

Idealism is by its nature dedication to the impossible. The idealist is often tempted to sacrifice the best possible for hope of the best imaginable. He or she should not be condemned for clarity of purpose or for this very human error. Yet the ideal will more nearly be achieved by resisting the temptation. It is frequently better to also be the pragmatist, to seek and secure the best available or the best consensus or the best first steps in the direction of the ideal.

Immigration

The ancestral home of nearly everyone in America is somewhere else. We all came here looking for a better opportunity and we found it. More than that we each brought our ingenuity and our labor and made America an even better place.

Most of us were not pretty when we arrived. America and Liberty said, "Give me your tired, your poor, your huddled masses yearning to breathe free, the wretched refuse of your teeming shore. Send these, the homeless, tempest-tost to me, I lift my lamp beside the golden door!" And we came. How many of us took a new name or a new spelling of our name because the clerk at Ellis Island could not speak our language and we could not speak his?

According to the International Organization for Migration, there are currently 241 million international migrants in the world of which 25 to 30 million are unauthorized. Of these, nearly half are illegal or undocumented aliens in the United States. In each of the past several years we have deported fewer than 300,000 other than those captured during entry by the border patrol. This information tells us a great deal, both about the desirability of migrating to the United States and about our incompetence in enforcement of immigration law.

It feels very safe to write about immigration even in the midst of immigration reform debate. We are not seriously examining how to use twenty-first century technology to enforce existing laws. We are not discussing the core issue of welcoming immigrants and holding them accountable to our traditional expectations. The result of the current debate will be changes at the margins, not fundamental reform.

Lets begin with a startling but time proven premise. New human beings, be they babies or immigrants, are new long-term assets. They are worthy of investment and will enrich us all. This has been our history and should be our future.

We need to welcome immigrants, and help them to become productive. We need to recognize that some of the best immigrant contributors to our economy are already here illegally. They are here because we need their labor and they need our opportunity. They are illegal because we made it easy to be illegal and too difficult to be legal. We need to re-enforce the traditions that immigrants come here supported by sponsors and by their communities with a clear imperative to dive into our diverse and productive culture. We need to invite them to use the opportunities and liberties that we offer and become productive citizens. Ironically, this will take less government micromanagement and cost less than our current feckless approach.

Such a welcoming attitude cannot exist without a disciplined process, but it need not be complicated. A visitor comes into this country either with a planned departure date, or as an immigrant with the intent to stay. Over half of our illegal immigrants come into this country legally as visitors and over-stay their permission. If a visitor enters as only a visitor, and we follow through to verify departure as expected, we immediately stem half of our illegal immigration problem that gets little attention and has nothing to do with border security.

For the other half, mostly our neighbors who come here primarily to work, have we thought about opening our borders? In the European Union, cross border labor is not seen as different from other cross border (free) trade. Labor is permitted to flow with the market, to the benefit of all. Why is that such a bad idea for NAFTA countries?

The birth rate in America is falling rapidly, causing concerns about our long-term debt and prosperity. Limiting births has doomed Japan and China to a path toward economic stagnation. Limiting immigration can do the same to America. If we increased the number of immigrants we welcome by 300,000 per year, or about thirty percent, we would still be increasing our population at a lower rate than in any year prior to 1994. We would immediately gain more workers and more consumers and reduce the aging of our population. If we also cease favoring uncles, aunts, cousins and people from "underrepresented" geographies; we can instead favor those who come here from our neighbors or for education or with skills. We would substantially reduce shortages of skills and surplus of dependency in our immigrant population.

We could also welcome those already here who accept their responsibility without changing any requirements for citizenship. We could drop the specious linkage between tenure as a guest worker and entitlement to citizenship. We could also abandon the ridiculous and futile notion that a "Berlin Wall" along our southern border is a sufficient or even an American solution.

If a visitor, already here or not, desires to be an immigrant worker or a resident, why would he or she not need to pass a security examination and provide an affidavit from two or more citizens providing a positive reference and pledging their sponsorship? In turn, why would the immigrant not pledge to keep an immigrant picture ID in possession at all times, to renew it annually, to keep a current address on file with the Immigration Service and his sponsors, to file an annual tax return regardless of income and to diligently seek to become productive. Is it cruel or discriminatory to ask these pledges of our guests when they are requirements for every citizen who has any income and drives an automobile? It would be an incredibly simple first step to make the USICS number on the green card become the taxpayer ID.

If we opened our shores to immigrants faithful to this contract, could any immigrant who does not comply or who falsifies papers complain about immediate deportation forthwith, no excuses, no exceptions, no reentry, no citizenship for children born while illegal? Why wouldn't any employer that does not have a current copy of all employee identifications on file face stiff fines? Why would States not be required to identify immigration status on any drivers licenses issued? With these few simple and enforceable rules, drivers licenses, Social Security numbers, U.S. bank and credit accounts would not be available to aliens without immigration credentials. Safety net benefits such as welfare, unemployment, food stamps, free medical care etc. could have strict pre-defined limitations commensurate with the immigrant's commitment to become a productive citizen. The ultimate safety net for those who want it could be a ticket back to their home country.

This approach might have been difficult in the twentieth century, but we are now in the age of Big Data. It may seem harsh, but it is undeniably fair. If we make it easy for those who relish opportunity, we then make it far easier to identify and penalize those who do not play by the rules, or those who come to harm us. Immigration status and citizenship are not entitlements. The quid pro quo for citizenship is citizenship.

Inheritance

If we have great success in building a fortune that lasts beyond our lifetime, how should we answer the following two questions?

First, how much of that fortune, at the end of our life, do we owe to the great opportunity provided to us by living in a free market economy and under a pluralistic and democratic government?

Second, beyond providing our children with education, a personal network and capital to establish their own enterprise and family, is a larger bequest to them more likely to be a blessing or a curse?

We can predict without fear of error that in any sample there will be a wide variety of responses to both questions, proving conclusively that the real answer to both is, "Probably to some extent!"

Why then do we give an income tax exemption to all unrealized capital gains in estates, thus cancelling an existing obligation of the decedent to the state in favor of the heirs? Inheritance taxes are not a double tax, but rather a red herring of far less significance than this grand subsidy!

Integrity

Integrity is integral to your being, or it is not. There is no such thing as having integrity some of the time, or most of the time. Narrowing the definition of the truth to half of the truth is a bait and switch to a lie. If integrity is a matter of convenience then it is only a poor illusion. Candidates and politicians often feign immunity, but they above all should be accountable for truth to those they serve.

There are a few good clues we too often forget. Always put contracts in writing if only to be sure the agreement is understood, but never think a man's signature is more reliable than his handshake. Question if any other can trust a man who cannot be trusted by his wife. Realize that one who lies to oneself may not even be conscious when lying to others.

A favorite verse from my father's collection:

HONOR

I can listen to the braggart
Or the vagrant as he lies.
I can stand the strident huckster
With his tawdry merchandise.
But the one that gets my nanny
And the one I cannot bear
Is the asinine deceiver
Who will cheat at solitaire.

Islam

Recently I was asked if I thought American Muslims were anti-American. The tone of the question seemed to be pre-judging the politically correct answer to be, "Of course not!" My answer is that I would be much more comfortable if American Muslims were to denounce the many attacks on American principles and property over the past three decades in the name of Sharia or Jihad, and the call to murder non-Muslim western "infidels."

There is a great divide between the Muslim World and Western democracies. Islam in the Middle East is perhaps a mirror of Christianity in Europe in the late middle ages, when kings ruled states and popes ruled kings. Scholars were first and primarily theologians serving the Church. Heresy was punishable by death. Without open challenge to authority, Luther, Calvin, Locke, Voltaire and many other voices could never have been heard. Without the Reformation and Enlightenment, Christian kings and clerics would still be abusing power.

An overriding reality of Islam today is the authority of clerics. Islamic states have shown little interest in a free press or freedom of dissent. They speak of religious tolerance, but at best it is tolerance for inferiors. In truth we have witnessed wholesale evacuations of Christians and Jews from their homes throughout the Middle East because of their religious affiliation.

Qutb, a father to the Salafi movement is said to have profoundly influenced Osama bin Laden and Iranian Supreme Leader Ali Khamenei. He wrote in *The Future of This Religion*, "There is only one House of Islam, and that is precisely the one in which an Islamic state has been founded, and God's sharia rules, and the divine punishments are applied, and in which Muslims support each other. Aside from this, everything is the House of War, and the relationship of the Muslim with it is either war or peace based on a treaty with it." It is not clear how many worshipers of Islam agree with this position, but there is little debate among Islamic clerics. We may accurately view terrorists as a minority fringe of Islam. However, the mainstream of moral leadership within Islam views and teaches, "There is only one House of Islam, and that is precisely the one in which an Islamic state has been founded, and God's sharia rules, and the divine punishments are applied." This teaching gives permission and cover to jihadists. It puts Islam in opposition to democratic forces in their own countries. It puts nations governed by Islamic Clerics in opposition to democratic nations. When they speak of peaceful relations and tolerance of other religious beliefs, they are speaking of peace with inferiors on their terms. They do not participate in relationships with infidels as equals. Perhaps all Muslims do not share this view, but it is what they are all taught by their moral and spiritual leaders. This is a universal tenet of Islam much as The Apostles' Creed is universal to Christians.

During the Protestant Reformation and Enlightenment periods, many Christians gave their lives to reform a corrupt Church. Our country was founded by and has welcomed millions of Christians and Jews disenfranchised and threatened by European kings and others denying their right to religious freedom. It may be in that tradition that many Muslims have migrated here. Yet where are the voices of Muslims who respect freedom and the Golden Rule? Why are they silent? We hear no voice from American Islam condemning Sharia, terror, blood and destruction. Islam's most vocal leaders call for the destruction of nations of infidels including especially Israel and the United States. Where is the courage of Americans Muslims who do not agree? Where are those who will say, "Our view of Islam values the legal traditions, secular justice and respect for individual freedom America guarantees?" What possible motivation could we have not to be wary of all Islam without such a voice? America offers the opportunity for growth and reform in all its institutions. The silence of American Muslims is a problem and a lost opportunity that screams for a voice.

Jail

Jail is perhaps the most destructive of all possible institutions. We put people in jail, sometimes for long periods, often before they have been convicted of a crime. We disrupt their lives, put them in an abusive environment and remove their ability to work. Once convicted it is a statistical truth that most coming out of our prison system are more prone to crime than before they entered. Why then would we ever put any in jail unless we believe them beyond redemption?

Many years ago a tour guide at Williamsburg, VA gave this explanation of early colonial justice. Extended jail sentences, he explained, were considered cruel and unusual punishment. The colonial jury had four sentencing options. If the offense was minor and the prisoner contrite they could issue an admonition and pardon. If a stronger message was thought necessary to prevent repetition, the jury could sentence time in the stocks to shame the prisoner and advertise his delinquency. If repetition were a greater risk, the prisoner could be tattooed to forever alert the population. Failing all these, the final option was execution.

Whether strictly true or somewhat embellished, this tale provides a reflection of a time when justice was a community affair. Without longing for a shadow of the distant past it still may be worthwhile to look at our practices in its light.

The United States jail and prison population is over 2.2 million, more than 700 for every 100,000 population. This is the highest rate in the world. Higher than Russia, higher than South Africa, more than seven times the rate in any other major nation. We have quadrupled our prison population since 1980. Are we really that "criminal" a nation? Are we four times more criminal than three decades ago?

What do we accomplish by incarcerating a prisoner? The answer is we do little or nothing to help the inmate become a productive and honest citizen, we do a great deal to introduce young offenders to older and more serous criminals and we keep most incarcerated criminals off the street only temporarily.

How well do we use available technology to craft alternatives to incarceration? We chip our dogs. We chip our cars. We implant many devices including defibrillators and pacemakers. Tracking convicts electronically and providing counseling and supervision can be enabled by GPS and database technology. Should it not be more effective and less expensive to track and supervise most non-violent wrong doers while helping them to rejoin productive society?

Is it possible to run a vast and diverse prison system where prisoners have no power and where practices have little visibility, without corruption, abuse and injustice? We seem to believe that every time we fail to imprison a criminal, society fails to eliminate a risk. Yet we ignore the reality that every time we do imprison a citizen, society takes different but equally real and costly risks.

The solution is doubtless complex, but for now must we continue to expand a system of injustice for many? No doubt there will continue to be some or many "beyond redemption." Yet in the twenty first century many new things are possible. We could start by sentencing many to surgical insertion of a GPS chip allowing them to be monitored at all times with no bricks or mortar. In combination with a free incoming only cell phone on their person at all times continuous "Big Brother" like supervision could be tailored to the particular offender and offenses. Software could do much of the tracking and analysis. Perhaps some will see this as an intrusion more severe than incarceration. Would any really prefer to go to jail? Clearly some re-thinking and experimentation is in order.

Judgment

Intelligence is the ability to learn and understand, the ability to process and apply logic or reason to complex combinations of information. But intelligence alone can be easily confounded when supplied with incomplete or conflicting information and stressed under the pressure of time constraints. These conditions, of course, apply to nearly every important or difficult decision where intelligence is most crucial.

Picture the golden retriever standing ready at her master's side. The Frisbee is tossed. Before the release the dog is at a full run, and in what seems a single motion captures the disc in mid flight. Now picture the aeronautical engineer, in the same position in possession of all the data and equations to calculate the position for a perfect catch. If that were possible, the equations are to complex and the action too fast for the engineer to duplicate the retriever's feat. He might succeed in catching the Frisbee, but only by disregarding equations and using his knowledge as a supplement to judgment derived from experience.

Judgment is the skill of sorting out important inputs from those less so. It is the talent to know when to make assumptions and when to gather more data. It is the perception to isolate cause from effect. It is the integrity to prioritize the truth over the desired conclusion. Modest intelligence used with good judgment and aimed forcefully toward a clear purpose is the driver of human history. Superior intelligence without judgment is a high-risk academic exercise. This is why there are so many taxi drivers with PhDs in New York and Boston. It is why there is a low correlation between Mensa membership and financial or professional success. It also explains why public policy should not be left to professors and why our greatest leaders are not necessarily the most "intelligent" ones.

Justice

Webster defines Justice; "The impartial adjustment of conflicting claims or the assignment of merited rewards or punishments... The establishment or determination of rights according to the rules of Law or Equity."

As our nation and government have grown, and as we have seen the need for more and more complex regulation we have assembled an awesome prosecutorial force to root out political corruption, extortion, insider securities trading, drug dealing, organized and disorganized crime and obedience to regulations.

The Department of Justice is not the only resource, but it is the centerpiece. It operates with many other federal agencies and provides leadership and collaboration to all the states. The DOJ spends $27 billion annually, of which $14 billion is for investigation and prosecution activities. It is so effective that more than ninety-five percent of the cases it brings to a conclusion are settled with plea bargains. This record is worthy of applause, perhaps tempered by a moral dilemma.

A 300-pound bully approaches a 98-pound weakling in the schoolyard demanding, "Give me half your marbles or I will take them all!" What response would we expect?

Daily we read, "Company A pleads guilty to charges of doing bad stuff or violating regulations, without admitting guilt and will pay a huge fine." Or "Person B pleads guilty to criminal activity without admitting guilt in exchange for a fine and a short sentence. The U.S. Attorney had charged B, asking for a larger fine and longer sentence. Person B's attorney asserted her client's innocence."

In our tradition of "Innocent until proven guilty!" vigilance for justice must include vigilance against crime and against 300-pound bully prosecutors. When over ninety-five percent of resolved cases are pleas of "guilty without admitting or proving guilt" there is at least an indication that the scale of justice may be out of balance.

The response might be that prosecutors with scarce resources are careful to prosecute only the strongest and most important cases. Yet no charges have been brought against Long Term Capital Management or MF Global. Left undiscovered are the most egregious creators of individual fraudulent sub-prime mortgage applications that broke the banks. At the same time we vigorously prosecute big banks for sins of those they bailed out and jailed Martha Stewart for one trade that profited her nothing. It is a given that politics and public relations at times affect the selection of targets by prosecutors, making the scales of justice even more difficult to keep balanced.

In a free society, the core rule of Law and Equity, the basis for economic justice, must be that no man can take for himself that which belongs to another. Perhaps we should re-balance the scales, and call for federal and state prosecutors to pay defense expenses when their prosecutions are unsuccessful. The 300-pound bully prosecutor would then be more careful with his accusations and the innocent defendant would have the right to defend himself without going broke in the process.

Loss

We like to think of our lives as a continuum of growth and increasing security. The reality is, that every life, no matter how blessed or fortunate, is punctuated more than once by profound loss. Each loss creates a need to re-assess and re-start on a new and unfamiliar path. The path we choose at the moment of each loss is the real test of our lives and the real legacy we leave for our children.

In every life and every generation, there are common threads and also differences. I have often found valuable lessons in my father's losses.

Some losses come very early and steel us for others that are to follow. In his fourth or fifth year of life, my father, Roy Moffitt, lost his mother. I do not know exactly when, only that she had an untimely death. If he had any, Roy never revealed memories of his mother. The earliest childhood memory he ever shared was his father placing him on a bar and saying, "Set them up for the house on the boy!" Throughout his life, he had little use for either whiskey or taverns.

When Roy finished the eighth grade in 1903, the household included his father David, two younger siblings, David's second wife Phoebe and two half-brothers ages one month and six years. Roy's help was needed on the farm. His schooling was, by necessity, complete. During the first year working on the farm, Roy decided not to accept that loss of schooling opportunity. The following fall, he traveled 225 miles to Lima, Ohio, found lodging with strangers and enrolled in high school. He shifted the year of his birth date so he would be the same age as his class.

After graduation in 1908, he drove a borrowed Cadillac for his last visit to his father, stepmother and siblings.

After high school, he went to work on a surveyor's crew for the telephone company. He studied engineering at night, was promoted & moved to Minneapolis, briefly served in the Army Signal Corps and was promoted again to chief of maintenance for the telephone company in Macon, Georgia. In Macon, he joined the Rotary Club and discovered a whole new world of possibilities. He concluded that he wanted to work more with people and bigger ideas, less with machinery and maintenance. To him, much of the value of his fifteen years experience was lost. At the same time, for reasons never known to me, he and his wife were divorced. She and their young son Steve moved back to her family home in Minneapolis.

In 1923, alone and needing a new portfolio, he moved to Chicago where the economy was booming and started a new career selling. He sold for Army & Navy Stores and then for Stevens Davis Sales Letters and finally sold furnaces for L. J. Mueller and Company. In 1931 with the depression deepening, Mueller put all salesmen on straight commission. Roy saw this as the loss of all security and support at an impossible time. He made a new choice. With only $100 in cash and no credit he secured contracts installing air conditioning in pavilions at the World's Fair opening the following year. The business was successful, grew and thrived. He secured a professional engineering license, broadened into design and building of industrial drying systems, married my mother, had three children and moved to the suburbs. Life was good.

Then in 1939 his son Steve, committed suicide. I cannot say how or if one can ever deal with a loss such as this. I only know that from that time forward, which was from my birth forward, my father carried with him a very private sadness and guilt and fear that made him dominate my life, mostly but not always to my benefit.

Then he became ill. He suffered terribly from stomach ulcers. He ate baby food and still had frequent bleeding. In 1947, his doctor told him to get out of his business; the worry and stress were killing him. If he continued he would be dead within one year. With the availability of antibiotics and private capital today the story would have taken a different turn, but panic struck. He sold the Moffitt Company to his key people for a share of earnings over three years. He sold his home and moved to Mississippi where his farm, initially bought as a hobby and tax shelter, became his only source of income. His children were 9, 12 and 13 years old when they arrived to start school in 1948.

Roy studied and practiced the best methods in scientific farming. Even so, the farm did not produce enough income, so he supplemented where he could. He managed a second farm for an absentee owner. He started the American Tung Oil Exchange and quickly became the broker of choice for most of the American Tung oil crop. He became a big fish in a very small pond for a short time until price supports sent the entire crop to the U.S. Department of Agriculture. He consulted with the Defense Department on drying foods for military rations in Korea. He built smokehouses for a local meat packer. He got along, and we got along. We lived nicely and did not think of ourselves as rich or poor. We were always taught not to waste, but never knew there was nothing to waste.

Then in 1957 my mother decided to leave my father. The reasons are another story, not important to this one. My two sisters were in college. I was a junior in high school. My mother was moving back to Chicago. She needed my moral support for survival. My father did not. So I moved to Chicago with my mother and my father once again lost both home and family. That loss of family was my first great loss.

Roy still got along. He built a small cottage for himself. He worked with the Masons, Boy Scouts, Job's Daughters, published a book of poems that he called doggerel, wrote a letter to his three children nearly every week, visited them when he could, and continued operating the farm. He hated debt, but borrowed on the farm for as long as he could, until he had to sell it in 1965 at age 76. This was a loss of his lifetime dream of leaving a section of land to his children as his grandfather had done. Four years later Hurricane Camille rolled over his home taking his life and all his possessions. Two hours before the storm hit, he declined to leave, telling me by phone that, "If my house goes, I will go with it!" The loss of my father was my second great loss, compounded by an unresolvable uncertainty if he gave up.

I saw my father deal with great losses and heard stories of others, all of which set a standard of expectations for myself. He taught by example to relish every moment, to prepare for adversity, and when it comes to have the resilience and fortitude to press on. When I told my wife Brenda this story, she said, "I don't think he was so unusual!" That is precisely my point. Many of our forbearers crossed an uncharted ocean and then an uncharted continent. They fought depressions and wars. They frequently lost everything or gave up everything only to set out on new paths. They needed, sought and found help along the way. That path of uncertainty, loss and recovery is neither an easy nor an avoidable price for freedom.

Michael Moffitt

Love

Love is not a consuming physical sensation. That would be lust. Love is not a rush of testosterone or adrenalin. That too would be lust or perhaps fear. Love is not the need to possess. That would be selfishness and conceit. Love is not the opposite of hate. Love and hate often co-exist. Indifference and selfishness are the opposites of love.

Love can be in the moment, an impulse, a compulsion or commitment to give. It can be an impulse to make another happy or to open another's life to new possibilities. One can honestly say "I love you" in this moment without looking before or beyond this moment. Love can also be forever, but love forever is not something fallen into. It is a commitment, an act of the human will. It is a decision to give oneself entirely and to give whatever is in our power to give, unconditionally and forever, no matter what other forces or feelings intervene. This is the love we give to a parent or a child or a spouse. This love is the core of happiness and the glue of civilization.

Michael Moffitt

Love

Love is not a consuming physical sensation. That would be lust. Love is not a rush of testosterone or adrenalin. That too would be lust or perhaps fear. Love is not the need to possess. That would be selfishness and conceit. Love is not the opposite of hate. Love and hate often co-exist. Indifference and selfishness are the opposites of love.

Love can be in the moment, an impulse, a compulsion or commitment to give. It can be an impulse to make another happy or to open another's life to new possibilities. One can honestly say "I love you" in this moment without looking before or beyond this moment. Love can also be forever, but love forever is not something fallen into. It is a commitment, an act of the human will. It is a decision to give oneself entirely and to give whatever is in our power to give, unconditionally and forever, no matter what other forces or feelings intervene. This is the love we give to a parent or a child or a spouse. This love is the core of happiness and the glue of civilization.

Luck

Luck is not a random or magical occurrence. Luck is preparation meeting opportunity.

Luck and love are both very much like farming. First the field must be prepared, opened and nourished to receive the seeds. When the seeds germinate, the farmer must recognize and nurture the valuable crops and remove the noxious weeds. Only after long and largely unnoticed labor does Nature provide the bountiful harvest of food or luck or love.

Marriage

The roots of marriage date to the origins of man. The lengthening of dependency of human infants created a dependency of mothers on fathers for the survival of our species. Throughout Man's history, the institution of marriage and the nuclear family have remained at the core of most religions and essential to the development of all advancing civilizations.

Marriage gives children a huge competitive advantage in life. Initially that advantage was survival. Today, data on educational and financial success are conclusive, but not necessary. Who would question that children growing up with the example and resources of two parents dedicated to them and to each other have a huge advantage over those who do not.

Something began to change in America in the mid twentieth century. In 1920 the marriage rate in the United States was 12.0 per 1,000 in our population. The divorce rate was 1.6. That year we consummated a net of 10.4 successful marriages per thousand people. In 1940, after a decade of boom and irresponsibility and another of depression and recession, the marriage rate was 12.1 and the divorce rate was 2.0. We were still consummating 10.1 successful marriages per thousand in our population each year. Grounds for divorce, except in Nevada, were usually limited to adultery or cruelty. When an unmarried girl got pregnant the expected outcomes were marriage to the father or giving the baby up for adoption.

In the early 1960s, the marriage rate hovered around 10.0 and the divorce rate around 2.5. Divorce was becoming easier. Births to un-wed mothers had grown to 5.3 percent of all births in 1960. However, we were still adding over 7.0 successful marriages per thousand in our population through 1970.

Then change accelerated. In 2002 for the first time, the successful marriage rate fell below 4.0. In 2009 the marriage rate was 6.8 and the divorce rate 3.5 setting a new record low of 3.3 net successful marriages per thousand people. In seventy years we had abandoned a cultural commitment that cradled our civilization for over four millennia. We had reduced the frequency of successful marriages by nearly two thirds. We had impoverished a wide swath of our nascent population, not from lack of material resources, rather from lack of the competitive advantage of a two-parent family. In 2005, 38.6 percent of all births in America were to un-wed mothers, over six times the rate of four decades earlier.

What has happened to our values and our culture that has so diluted the strength of our commitment to family life? Why have so many abandoned commitments to marriage and the nuclear family? Is it any wonder that we are developing an underclass of uneducated children who began without a nuclear family? Is it a surprise that these children face a competitive disadvantage, or that escape from the underclass is difficult? Are these children wrong to feel they have unequal opportunity? Would they be wrong to feel angry? What can be done to help them? What can be done to help the next generation of unborn children?

There are no simple answers, yet two observations are clear. First, in 1980, twenty years after the collapse of our collective commitment to marriage, our prisons began to overflow beginning a quadruple expansion of inmate population in two decades. There surely is a connection.

Second, and perhaps more important, it seems that we are losing the joy and the profit of marriage. Too many do not seem to understand the joy of two people fully committed to one another, the communion of giving self to one another, of sharing body and spirit alone and with no others. Too many do not seem to grasp the simple leverage of two people able to count on one another unconditionally; leverage that gives them competitive advantage in their every endeavor, especially in the raising of children. Perhaps it is time to put selling the benefits of personal commitment and responsibility in marriage at the top of our social agenda.

Medicine

Fortunately, I have not had a lot of personal experiences that have made me think medical care in America is completely broken. Equally fortunate for my readers, I have no illusion that I have all or even many of the answers. However, given experience to date both before and since the Affordable Heath Act, it seems reasonable to hope that our Health Care Policy is still a work in process.

I look to doctors who are also granddads for insight. One says, "I remember calling on a patient with my father (also a doctor). Right away it was clear she had pneumonia." There was no insurance, and she pleaded, "Please doctor, can you treat me at home?" "So we called for some penicillin. In a few days she was better and the whole thing cost $25. Today the ambulance, emergency room, tests, MRI, and hospital room could easily cost $25 thousand." There are many such stories that illustrate three principles that should be part of any conversation.

The first is that no medical care system can work well without a relationship of trust between doctor and patient. To deny that relationship or degrade it by denigration or bureaucratic muddle is to damage health care for all.

The second principal is that if people do not understand costs and can treat a service as free, the service will be overused, wasted and will rapidly become more expensive. This is true of any product or service. It's inevitably leads to the conclusion that not everyone wants or needs or can afford the same medical insurance. The more choices people have, the more knowledgeable they will be about costs. The more they participate in those costs, the better they will understand the cost and risk relationships. The result of greater understanding and participation will be better cost management and greater value as defined by consumers in the marketplace. The underlying truth is that there is simply no possibility for unlimited free medicine for all.

Finally, if the government is inclined to protect consumers, the single protection that is most needed is a requirement that, once a person is insured, that insurance policy is a commitment from the insurer to cover the insured for life. This is not trivial, as it would require portability from state to state, from group to individual policies, and from dependent to single insured and later to newly insured household status. However it is clearly a feasible requirement. It is already a requirement for life and long term care insurance.

If we formulate a national approach to medical care beginning with these three foundations, we have a chance for building consensus and success.

Some say we should have Medicare for all. I am a very appreciative customer of Medicare, but it disqualifies itself on three counts. First, it has begun interfere with doctor patient relationships via price controls that are forcing doctors out of the system.

Second, Medicare accounting is opaque. Of all the services I use, including banking, investments, utilities, credit accounts and even my dry cleaner, Medicare is the only one that does not provide monthly statements showing what services have been provided, what they cost and what has been paid. For most credit accounts we get such statements either on paper or on line. They help us to understand what we have spent and to avoid fraud and errors. Medicare provides no such insights. The paperwork they send is not timely and often not clearly related to services and never summarized. It is no wonder with this lack of information management that fraud and abuse is a problem.

This leads to the third disqualification of Medicare as a model. Estimates of costs due to Medicare fraud and abuse, even estimates by the federal government, range upwards from 20 percent or nearly $200 billion annually. No private enterprise could or would tolerate abuse approaching that magnitude. Unless those costs can be controlled, Medicare, or any federally provided medical insurance cannot be rationally considered as part of an economical solution. If these costs become demonstrably controlled, our experience with Medicare might be useful in a discussion of where we go from here.

Meditation

Meditation is the process of reaching into the depth of our inner self and leaving behind all externalities. It is perhaps the most powerful of all human activities. It begins as calisthenics for the soul, by learning and practicing complete absorption in the self and in the moment. It builds the strength and skill to exercise our powers of observation and will to higher levels. It enables inner peace and defeats stress and distraction.

In its ultimate meditation enables total concentration and focus on the self and the exercise of will over the self. Through it we can achieve focused visualization of our being as we will it to be; complete absorption in the moment without reference to past or future or external space or limitations. Through meditation we can accomplish miracles that astound ourselves and that science has yet to explain.

My nephew's wife Peggy was trying to conceive a child through in-vitro fertilization. Her doctor implanted fertilized eggs and suggested that she visualize them attaching themselves into the wall of her uterus. As she did, she pictured three eggs nestling as though in a shag rug, and a fourth floating, without settling in. Thirty-two weeks later she delivered healthy triplets. She felt before her doctors told her that the forth egg was threatened and also that the other three had found nourishment. Her vision included individual differences among the triplets, some to be verified after birth. Perhaps this was coincidence or hope or perhaps her meditation influenced the outcome for the three healthy babies. I choose to believe her meditation allowed her to look inside herself, gather information and exert influence in ways we do not fully understand. Her doctor apparently thought that a possibility as the visualization was his suggestion.

Michael Moffitt

When my wife Ann was diagnosed with brain cancer, we listened together to many tapes about meditation, and she took it seriously as part of her treatment. As her tumor was eating its way through her brain, it gradually robbed her of control of the left side of her body. An early manifestation was facial sagging resulting in drooling from the left side of her mouth. She was more stylish than that, and looked inside herself to find a fix. That was in July. By October she had lost all control and most feeling on her entire left side, except that her face was in near perfect balance and remained so from late July until she died in November. This was the most dramatic of several repairs Ann was able to make to improve her life while her physical control was being devastated by cancer. Her doctors had no medical explanations.

There are many documented examples of the power of meditation, perhaps most notably the lamas in Tibet. I choose the examples of Peggy and Ann because these two women were not extensively schooled in meditation. They each found themselves in a situation where they needed to look intensively within themselves and find new resources. They are extraordinary women, not because they have extraordinary powers but because they used powers we all have in extraordinary ways. Each of us can find and use the power of meditation in our lives if we choose to do so.

Moderation

Moderation as a tactic or strategy has been applauded since Aesop's tale of the Tortoise and the Hare. Moderation is to take things deliberately or one step at a time; to make preparation before sprinting to the finish; to pause for mid-course corrections. Each or all can help to hit the target sooner or more squarely. Moderation of pace is often a necessity and almost always a virtue. The longer the journey, the more important is this maxim.

Moderation of purpose, however, is an oxymoron. What sense could it make to be moderately committed to winning the race or hitting a target?

In the political realm we often see moderate as a complimentary term, describing one who is willing to compromise, to work with those having differing views toward the greater good for all. Sometimes compromise is a good thing, but only if it contributes to a purpose. How do we take a moderate position on fighting or winning a war? What is the moderate point between justified and winnable or not? How can we be moderate about whether we will pay our debts? Should President Kennedy have been more moderate about removing Russian missiles from Cuba or landing a man on the moon in a decade? Should President Truman have been more moderate and not fire a defiant General McArthur? Should General Eisenhower have been moderate in the face of D-Day weather forecasts? Should President Lincoln have been more moderate about preserving the Union? Should we have inserted "moderate" in each article of the Bill of Rights? Is it a compliment to be described as moderately attractive or having moderate integrity?

In the political theater the most hurried and least moderate often describe those who disagree as divisive partisans. The key to understanding this theater is that the radical usually prefers to act in haste while the real moderate prefers not to repent at leisure.

Native Americans

Most Americans feel more than a tinge of guilt for the extermination of nine million or so Native Americans through brutality and disease accomplished in the process of developing and organizing our nation. Unfortunately, too few of us focus on the theft and fraud visited upon the 240,000 that remained alive in 1887 and their descendants. This is perhaps as egregious a chapter, and with no possible excuses related to the clash of civilizations or Manifest Destiny.

In 1798, the United States government began a policy of recognizing the sovereignty of American Indian Nations and codifying treaties with them that preceded the United States Constitution. Under these treaties, millions of acres in the contiguous United States were recognized as property retained for or by Indian Nations. Because the United States government did not consider the tribes capable of managing their affairs, the land was placed in government-controlled reservations. Additional treaties were made as the nation moved westward, with the "reserved" land growing to 138 million acres.

In 1871 Congress declared that no further treaties would be made with Indian Nations and all future dealings with them would be handled through legislation and without negotiation. In 1887 Congress passed the General Allotment Act, otherwise known as the Dawes Severalty Act. This Act confirmed that Congress had the right to strip Indian tribes and Native Americans of lands reserved for them over nearly a century of treaties without their agreement and without due process. This Act and others that followed in 1902, 1906 and 1908 along with administration of their provisions by the Bureau of Indian Affairs stripped the Indian Nations of their sovereignty and over 78 million acres of their birthright. Another 10 million acres were allotted to individual Native Americans, some of whom were vested with ownership of small plots 25 years hence. The language used to justify this pillage included, "To help the Indians assimilate into our culture!" and "Disposing of lands surplus to Indian needs!" and "Indians were declared incompetent to handle their land affairs, so the United States needed to retain legal title to the land as trustee."

In 1934 The Indian Reorganization Act or Wheeler-Howard Act ended the land allotments and retained all individual and tribal lands in trust, controlled by the Bureau of Indian Affairs in perpetuity. In an irony of Orwellian scale, sovereignty of Indian Nations was limited to those lands held in trust and completely controlled by the government, but with no accountability to the Indians.

Since that time, many Native Americans and members of Congress have complained about this lack of accountability. GAO audit reports in 1928, 1952 and 1955 highlighted fraud and un-auditable accounts, but did not result in reform. After a decade of pressure from Congress in the 1980s, the Bureau of Indian Affairs engaged Arthur Anderson accountants to perform a complete audit of trust accounts. The auditors reconciled 2000 tribal accounts for the period of 1973 to 1992, reporting that at least $2.4 billion was unaccounted for and billions more were virtually untraceable because of incomplete government records. The auditors also reported they were unable to reconcile the 17 thousand Individual Indian Money Accounts in trust because the government had not maintained sufficient records. The report compiled by the House Committee on Government Operations was titled, "Misplaced Trust: The Bureau of Indian Affairs' Mismanagement of the Indian Trust Fund." No reform resulted from the report.

In 1996, Elouise Cobell, a member of the Blackfeet tribe from Browning, Montana, and a bank employee in Bozeman, Montana brought suit against the United States Government for mismanagement of Indian lands and failure to pay royalties for generations. Damages were thought to be in the range of $10 to $40 billion.

Mrs. Cobell's suit was not about reparations. It was about breach of fiduciary trust. Much of the wealth built in our nation in the eighteenth and nineteenth centuries was built with land as the principal producing asset. Agriculture, timber, mining, oil and gas all were and still are the source of great fortunes. Yet Native Americans did not prosper with their birthright of 138 million acres. Of the 4.5 million descendants, over one million still live on reservations with per capita annual incomes of $7,000 and a life expectancy of fifty years. These Native Americans did not fritter away the profits from their land and timber and minerals. They had the wisest and most powerful government in the world looking after their interests.

Elouise Cobell's suit became a class action on behalf of 300,000 Native Americans.

It is not easy to sue the United States Government. For thirteen years the government delayed, denied, obfuscated and offered token settlements. In February 1999 Federal Judge Royce Lamberth held Interior Secretary Bruce Babbitt and Treasury Secretary Robert Rubin in civil contempt for, "flagrant disregard for the orders of this court and the defendants' corresponding lack of candor in concealing their wrongdoing." Judge Lamberth imposed fines and appointed a special master to oversee document production in the case. The case still languished for another decade. Finally, in December 2009 the U. S. Government agreed to pay $3.4 billion,

"To right a century of wrongs that cheated Indians out of the proceeds from their properties." Of this settlement, $2 billion was used to purchase individual plots of land that had passed through many generations of estates and thereby close out many of the Individual Money Accounts without accounting for decades of lost revenues. The remaining $1.4 billion was a negotiated and discounted compensation well short of the specific losses the Anderson audit definitively identified fifteen years earlier.

Eloise Corbel felt the settlement fell short of what was owed for, "The largest case of fiscal mismanagement on behalf of citizens in U.S. history." President Obama called it, "an important step towards reconciliation." Interior Secretary Ken Salazar said, "With the settlement now final, we can put years of discord behind us and start a new chapter in our nation-to-nation relationship."

This new chapter includes no penalties, no interest, no acknowledgement of malfeasance by the government, no commitment to manage the trusts differently, foreclosure of any settlement for seven hundred thousand Native Americans still living on reservations and other tribal members not represented in the suit. The settlement continues the premise that, "Indians are incompetent to handle their land affairs, so the United States needs to retain legal title to their land as trustee." The new chapter as now being written perpetuates over one hundred twenty-five years of theft, fraud and incompetence by the Bureau of Indian Affairs.

Wouldn't a more satisfying new chapter begin with emancipation of Native Americans and giving the tribes clear title to the remaining fifty-six million "reserved" acres that have not been pilfered? The requirement of the title transfer could be to corporations or partnerships or whatever structures each tribe chooses, so long as the ownership and control accrues to every individual member of the tribe. Individual Native Americans need not be compelled to trade one "blind trustee" for another. Without the land "trusts" the tribes would no longer need the fiction of "sovereignty." Native Americans could become full citizens and vested in their birthright. Best of all, the Bureau of Indian Affairs could be terminated, no longer having anything to steal or mismanage and no longer costing taxpayers a $2.6 billion budget each year to do so.

Paradise

The word "paradise" comes from Persian roots meaning a walled garden. It evokes the image of Adam and Eve romping in the Garden of Eden. Yet frequently we forget the importance of the wall, the limits that preserve paradise. The Garden of Eden ceased to be a paradise when Adam ignored the one single limit.

We all see the need for laws to limit anti-social behavior, rules to provide discipline for our children and contracts to define our business and personal relationships. It is equally true, if perhaps less obvious, that each of us can create and sustain our personal paradise only when we respect the limits that allow those around us to create and sustain theirs.

It is fundamental to teachings of all religions that complete freedom brings no paradise or peace, only chaos. Otherwise we would need no authority of God, no concept of sin, no requirement for prayer or meditation or atonement.

It is fundamental to all interactions among citizens or within families that trust and happiness can be enjoyed only when we live within mutually accepted limits.

Perseverance

Calvin Fenner was born in 1819 in Henrietta, New York. Few records remain of the details of his life or possessions, but there are enough to tell his story. In 1823, Rochester, eight miles to the north of Henrietta, had a population of 2,500 residents. The Erie Canal opened between Albany and Buffalo in 1825. The combination of proximity to the canal and the waterfalls in the Genesee River to power mills made Rochester an early boomtown. By 1834 Rochester had a 13,500 residents, twenty mills on the Genesee and was shipping 44,000 tons of flour annually to Albany and New York City.

Calvin grew up at the edge of this boom in modest prosperity. He married Elizabeth Wilcox, and their first child, Bradford Clark Fenner, was born on June 29, 1849. Calvin was 30, Elizabeth was 25, and it was time for them to seek their fortune.

The New York and Erie Railroad opened in 1851. The one hundred fifteen mile trip from Rochester, to the western terminus in Dunkirk, New York took only eight hours, offering the opportunity to scout the area and plan the first leg of their journey westward. In 1852, Calvin, Elizabeth and Bradford moved to Chautauqua, New York, twenty-seven miles southwest of Dunkirk. There they tested their skills at frontier agriculture. The following year the Galena and Chicago Union Railroad opened between Chicago and Galena, Illinois, offering better access to more fertile land to the west. At the break of spring in 1855 Calvin and Elizabeth made their irrevocable commitment to the frontier. They traveled thirty-eight miles westward to Erie, PA, where they boarded The Lake Shore and Michigan Southern Railway to Chicago. About ten days and 720 miles later, they arrived in Galena, IL across the Mississippi River from Dubuque,

Iowa. Ten years earlier, this trek would have taken over a month and involved much greater hardship.

Their planned destination was Manchester, Iowa, sixty miles farther west. Provisions had to be secured. A wagon was required to get to their new home, as well as to carry future provisions and bring products to market. Tools were required for farming and for building a cabin. Food staples, supplies and seed were required. At least a horse, mule or ox was needed to pull the wagon and later till the soil. A large canvas tarp would protect their cargo, and be used as a tent top until they could build shelter. Calvin and Elizabeth may have brought funds for these things, or they may have partnered with one or more other families along the way or by pre-arrangement. Many such partners would become neighbors for life, so these were important decisions. That year, 175,000 settlers entered Iowa, mostly ferrying across the Mississippi River from Galena to Dubuque or from Rock Island, Ill. to Davenport, Iowa. Consequently, there was no shortage of partner candidates and this is not just Calvin and Elizabeth's story.

One final stop, after ferrying across the river was the land office in Dubuque. By 1851, all of the Indian lands in northern Iowa were in the hands of white men, mostly the U. S. government. Registration there was not required to establish a homestead, but much valuable information about law, surveys and ownership was available. It was a wise stop, especially since Iowa had been granted statehood in 1846.

The final sixty miles of their journey was by trail, and with luck could take as few as three days. It frequently took much longer. Small amounts of rain could swell streams and cause backups at fords. Frequently, storms would transform the trail into a muddy quagmire with deep ruts making progress impossible. Many of us have seen storms through our windshields that make us hide under an overpass. Imagine passing through such a storm with a five year old son and all your possessions in an open wagon with only a tarp to crawl under for shelter!

Manchester, Iowa was a fledgling town, founded in 1850. Upon their arrival Calvin and Elizabeth needed to select land, have it surveyed and begin building their future. Before they could do any planting, a prairie plow contractor was hired to open the prairie matted deep with grass roots undisturbed for centuries. They had roughly six months to establish their farm, build a cabin and lay in fuel and supplies for the following winter.

Calvin and Elizabeth lived on their farm, worked hard and prospered there until they died, he in 1891 and she in 1909. They saw young Bradford grow up, get married, raise five children, take over the farm operations and become a leader in the community. They never owned a tractor, or had running water, electricity, radio or telephone. Elizabeth never had fancy clothes or cosmetics, but she was always beautiful in Calvin's eyes.

I have long admired Calvin and Elizabeth as embodiments of perseverance. In their odyssey to Iowa and in their life there they always did whatever it took to continue the journey. Perseverance is the act of persistence. It is being steadfast. It is not waiting or depending upon others to move ahead or to catch us when we fall. It is essential to succeeding in any but the most trivial enterprise. The more worthwhile or necessary the enterprise, the more essential perseverance becomes. For Calvin and Elizabeth it was essential to existence, theirs and all their children and children's children including until today and including mine. Calvin's oldest granddaughter Bertha was my grandmother.

Human history would have been very dull and probably very short without perseverance. Every life is richer when its owner perseveres toward its fulfillment and eschews excuses. What a shame it would be to forget this lesson or to teach otherwise.

Ponzi Scheme

Carlo Pietro Giovanni Guglielmo Tebaldo Ponzi was born on March 3, 1882 in Lugo, Italy. He arrived in Boston on November 3, 1903 with $2.51 in his pocket. Late in 1919 after an unimpressive career that included jail terms in Montreal and Atlanta, he began the "Business" that would make his name famous.

Ponzi promised huge returns on investments in international postal coupons. He delivered these returns, as much as 100 percent in 90 days, paid with money received from new investors. There were no real investments. Payments to investors could only be made as long as new money came in. And it did come in, by the millions, until it collapsed and Ponzi surrendered to federal authorities on August 12, 1920.

Estimates of the total fraud and losses vary. Ponzi was quoted from his last interview nearly thirty years later, "Even if they never got anything for it, it was cheap at that price. Without malice aforethought I had given them the best show that was ever staged in their territory since the landing of the Pilgrims! It was easily worth fifteen million bucks to watch me put the thing over."

Ponzi was not the first, nor the last to impoverish "greedy" investors with promises of impossible returns. He was for a long while the most outlandish. Yet right in front of our eyes are schemes that dwarf Ponzi and even dwarf the more recently famous Madoff. These schemes are no secret, and will not collapse as rapidly as Ponzi or Madoff, but collapse they surely will.

When you or I invest in a pension annuity, or when we participate in a company pension plan, law requires that the pension fund

111

retain assets sufficient to pay off its obligations. A corporation or insurance company must carry its pension promises on its books as liabilities and must have assets set aside to meet these obligations. Any pension manager who does not account this way is likely to enjoy the hospitality of a federal prison. This is not, however, the way government accounting works. Governments, like Ponzi, only talk about current cash transactions.

The Social Security Trust fund contained $2.7 trillion at the end of 2011. These funds were all invested in U.S. Government Bonds, backed by the full faith and credit of the United States Government. Yet the estimated present value of liabilities for future Social Security pension and disability payments exceeds $20 trillion. Even the $2.7 trillion "invested" in bonds by the trust fund has been spent, just as Ponzi did with his investor's money. The bonds can still be redeemed only because the asset behind the bonds is the Government's ability to print money or raise your taxes.

At www.socialsecurity.gov under Trust Fund Frequently Asked Questions, the authors ask, "Why do some people describe the "special issue" securities held by the trust funds as worthless IOUs? What is SSA's reaction to this criticism?"

It seems incredible that the question should be asked and highlighted in bold type on the Social Security website. The answer is illuminating: "Many options are being considered to restore long-range trust fund solvency. These options are being considered now, over 20 years in advance of the year the funds are likely to be exhausted. It is thus likely that legislation will be enacted to restore long-term solvency, making it unlikely that the trust funds' securities will need to be redeemed on a large scale prior to maturity." In plain English, "Yes we are going broke. To avoid doing so we are looking at options to raise taxes or to reduce benefits or to print more money."

The problem is not twenty years away. It is now. During the 1990s, the trust fund grew at a compound annual rate of 15.1 percent due to contributions by baby boomers greater than benefits paid to their less populous parents. In 2011, the fund grew 2.7 percent. It is no longer growing. Beginning now, benefits are greater than payroll taxes and additional funding will be required each year from additional debt or increased taxes. It is only a small amount at first, just $100 billion or so. Most baby boomers will be retiring during the next twenty years. The population of this age group is 10 percent greater than the current retirees, meaning a 10 percent increase in cost of benefits. Life expectancy in the past 20 years increased from 75 years (eight years after retirement) to 78 years (eleven years after retirement), another 35 percent increase in benefit term. Meanwhile, the work force is shrinking. These demographic changes, resulting in at least a 50 percent increase in benefits to be financed by each worker in the labor force, are powering us toward at least a $250 billion annual deficit within this decade. It does not matter when the Trust Fund goes broke. Until it goes broke, we must borrow to pay the shortfall of benefits vs. payroll taxes. After it goes broke, we still will borrow and increase taxes to pay the shortfall of benefits vs. payroll taxes. This will continue forever, until it ends. The same is true of military pensions and many state employee pension funds.

According to the Medicare trustees' report, the present value of unfunded liabilities for promised Medicare payments is $42.8 trillion. Future taxes and borrowings will be required to cover all of those commitments plus interest. This does not matter. We will borrow and increase taxes to pay the shortfall of benefits vs.

payroll taxes. This will increase with Obamacare and it too will go on forever, until it ends.

It is instructive to note that, while we speak of a $16 trillion national debt, a corporation with the same liabilities would be required to report liabilities of at least $79 trillion. Who knows how many more such pension and benefits liabilities are hidden from the balance sheets of states, municipalities, school districts and other local government agencies? Who knows when the burden of these debts will suffocate our economy and bankrupt our children and grandchildren? The question is not whether, but when, unless we face the problem and look today for the least bad solution. There may still be time to find it.

Poverty

Poverty is by definition an unsolvable problem. Those among us with the least are by definition the poor. No one believes it matters that our poor have wealth and incomes over 100 times greater than the poor in China or India. No one proposes that we give our resources to Asia so their poor can be as rich as our poor. What matters is that our poor are poor by local standards of today.

Poverty is not a social or cultural problem. It is a natural characteristic of any culture. When we try to eliminate poverty, we take on a Sisyphean challenge. No matter how much we help the poor, no matter how much we give them, there will still be those with the least and they will be, "the poor."

We will continue to be frustrated in our battle to end poverty because we continue to misunderstand the meaning and purpose of safety nets. A safety net is a means of breaking a fall. It is a means to save the life of one who has jumped or fallen from a building or a trapeze. Once saved, the person in the safety net must immediately get off to allow the next person to be saved. The safety net does not care why the person jumped or fell, whether or not they are injured or whether they are likely to fall again. At the edge of the safety net is a human being with an outstretched hand. That person who cares, not the safety net, helps the fallen person to rise again.

Our poverty programs are not safety nets. They are places to live; weekly funding for food, shelter, childcare and other benefits that become entitlements designed to raise the platform upon which poverty resides. Too few address the individual. Too few confront the individual with his or her responsibility on the path to a better place, or encourage them to take that path.

Children in poverty are often equated with hopelessness only because we do not think of the individual child. This can be said with confidence since the individual child's solution is quite simple. If the outstretched hand that reaches the child in poverty persuades that child to finish high school, and until then to obey the law and to refrain from breeding, that child will have anted up in the high stakes game of seeking the Great American Dream. This is a guarantee, not a guarantee of finding the dream. It is a guarantee of not finding the dream if you are not in the game. What parent would not teach their child this lesson? What friend would not teach it? What teacher or employee of our government would not teach it?

All that is required for an individual child to escape poverty is for the child and its support group to take personal responsibility to achieve those three simple goals. This was true when I was a child and is true today. A safety net can do many things, but any safety net that does not include an outstretched hand and focus on helping each individual to become more productive and self reliant is a futile waste of resources, perhaps even a negative force.

If we parse all the causes for poverty or all the groups in poverty we will find one common thread. For all save the mentally ill or inept, all the paths from poverty to self - sustenance require respect for the individual and commitment from the individual. Without that respect and commitment, all efforts for sustaining safety nets will only build and expand a permanent underclass.

Rape

Sex between consenting adults can be a business proposition, recreation, a communion, or any combination of the three. In an ideal world, it would always be a communion, a physical affirmation of a spiritual commitment, seasoned by recreation. But regardless of the relationship, adults are adults.

It is different in high school. Nearly every high school boy looks at sex as a conquest on his path to manhood. Even when he thinks he loves his girlfriend, he longs for her surrender. If an older boy or man has sex with a high school age girl, especially unprotected sex, how could it be less than abusive, or criminal?

In 2010, in the United States there were over 200,000 abortions performed on girls between ages 15 and 18 years. There were also 367,678 children born to girls between ages 15 and 19. Add these together and they amount to over 500,000 cases of high school age girls having sex with DNA evidence available to identify the father. These are only ones that resulted in pregnancy in a single year.

What more cruel crime can we imagine than relegating a teenage girl to a choice between having a child as a single mother or killing a new life within her. The reality is that for a moment of power and irresponsibility it happens more than ten thousand times each week in America.

"They were in love", they say, or" She wanted to have sex too." Why should there be consequences for the boy (or the man)? What about the consequences for the girls? Do we think these girls don't know the consequences? Hopefully they have mothers. Is it really possible that more than 500,000 high school age girls each year in America decide to risk so burdening their lives for a moment of passion or submission?

In 2010 in the United States, 85,593 cases of forcible rape were recorded in national crime statistics. Why do we even keep track of such a meaningless statistic? If we recognized high school age abortions and pregnancies as products of rape, there would be seven times that many.

Many things could be done to reduce this tragedy. We could require identification and responsibility of the father for aid to the mother and child. We could use pulpits or bully pulpits. We could cry out in horror! The silence is deafening!

Perhaps we should increase the legal age of statutory rape to 18 years from 16 years. We seem comfortable with strict limitations on sale of alcohol to or its consumption by children. Are not the issues of judgment of children identical? Are not the risks to children and to society at least comparable? If children drivers were causing 500,000 accidents with injuries every year, would we consider increasing the eligibility age for drivers? Do we believe children have "reproductive rights" without the ability to accept reproductive responsibilities? Should we tolerate sex among children or between adults and children? Are we so afraid of being prudish that we call these problems of abortion or teenage single parents? Those are symptoms. How can we not call the problem rape?

Regret

I do not believe in regret. Life is linear. To regret a decision or an event is to regret everything in life that follows. Every time a choice is made, everything that follows is changed by that choice. We tend to focus on what seem to be our biggest decisions and forget the importance of all the small ones. How often are our lives changed by blind fortune or a simple decision to be at the wrong place at the wrong time, or at the right place at the right moment? Regret is a foolish and wasteful emotion. It is as useless as wishing to un-ring a bell. This assertion in no way conflicts with the need to continuously look critically at one's life and learn to make better decisions. On the contrary, it encourages us to make large and small decisions with equal rigor and to always live looking forward.

Regulation

In the ninety years between 1910 and 2000 employment of accountants and auditors in the United States grew thirteen times in proportion to total employment. One could argue that business and financial affairs grew more complex in this period, but so did everything else. During the same period accountants also progressed from green eyeshades and hand written journals to computers, databases and the Internet. One would expect some measure of productivity improvement.

During the same ninety year period healthcare became more complex as well. We invented countless vaccinations and drugs including antibiotics and antihistamines and biotechnology. We invented modern surgery and organ replacement. We invented health insurance covering 86 percent of Americans by the year

2000. We increased our life expectancy by 50 percent. We increased healthcare employment by five times in proportion to total employment, about 60 percent less than the growth of accountants and auditors.

During the same period, the population of lawyers grew three times faster than physicians and surgeons. The annual cost to employ and support the growth of lawyers and accountants beyond the growth rate of doctors and other health professionals in the last century is estimated at about $1,000 per man woman and child in America, or three percent of personal income. In academic literature, there is little disagreement that regulations have driven the explosion of work for lawyers and accountants. Yet this is only the cost to keep score. The greater cost is that imposed by regulations on those who are regulated. The actual cost of understanding and complying with all government regulation including taxation, safety, ecological, banking, transportation, education, personnel and labor, food and packaging etc. dwarfs the cost to keep score.

Presidential orders and proclamations, federal rules and regulations and notices of hearings and meetings regarding regulations are published daily in the Federal Register. There was no perceived need for this publication prior to 1935. Today its volume is a staggering 85,000 pages annually.

It can be argued that every regulation fills a need or performs a useful function. But when we make that argument we must also ask, "Is this regulation understandable without an army of lawyers? Is the regulation enforceable? Will this regulation accomplish the desired result?" and "Is the likely result worth the cost of the regulation?" We should realize that the first best regulation is for transparent disclosure. The second level of regulation, if needed, should be elegant in its simplicity. For example, a requirement for higher levels of capital by banks reduces their exposure and the exposure of all their depositors to risk and reduces the risk of corruption to a far greater extent than thousands of detailed rules or requirements for continuing bureaucratic examinations and approvals. Overlapping and duplicate federal and state permitting authorities adds complexity in greater portion than effectiveness.

Our current process is the antithesis of elegance. We usually begin with an "important" threat or crisis. Our elected representatives authorize regulations. Bureaucrats, frequently those who failed to predict or prevent the crisis write the regulations. Bureaucratic staffs are increased to implement the regulations. Bureaucratic agendas frequently expand legislated imperatives. There are always unintended consequences and market distortions. There are almost never metrics to measure effectiveness.

Examples are too abundant to be necessary. Every dollar spent to impose a regulation, to conform to it and to keep score and enforce it is a tax on every citizen. Each of us as a citizen is paying these costs in addition to the taxes we pay to support the regulatory superstructure. We are paying these costs instead of feeding or educating our children, saving for our retirement, living in a nicer home, giving to charity, taking a vacation or however we as free citizens would use that income. If we prioritized transparency and simplicity, required a disciplined cost vs. benefit analysis, and automatically set sunset or review dates, the Federal Register would be much shorter and we all would be freer and richer people.

Religion

In what life have there not been breathtaking moments, moments when the overwhelming beauty of nature or insight is beyond description, moments when the wonder of life educes awe and gratitude? At such times, do not most mortals question how it is possible to experience such wonder?

In what life have there not been moments of loss, desperation and helplessness, moments when there seem no earthly solutions to our woe? What mortal has never questioned, "Am I not more than just this fragile body, do I just occupy this vessel and may perhaps later move on to some more perfect experience?" Who has ever told a child, "Granddad is dead and does not exist at all, anywhere any more?"

Throughout history the human reaction to these questions has frequently been to see God or Gods as a source of wonder, strength and consolation. In every civilization belief in God or Gods has become the source of spiritual awareness and moral framework, structure and discipline. These have enabled health, cooperation and survival for the human family.

Religion and family were the first organizational constructs in human civilization, preceding and laying the foundation for philosophy and law. Until recently on the calendar of man's progress, emperors and kings were deemed to be endowed by God. Rule of law and separation of church and state were fresh ideas at the time of America's founding. They are at best only hopeful forces in much of today's emerging world.

There are those who believe religion is obsolete in our modern world. Marx called it "the opiate of the masses." Our constitutional protection for freedom *to practice* religion has evolved for many to mean freedom *from exposure to* religion. Yet who really knows what intelligence is beyond our understanding? Who can claim to know all that can be known? Who knows what spirit if any survives this life, what form it takes or where it lives? Who has gone there and come back to inform us? If religion is to be replaced by science, how does science teach values or morality? Can science provide a vocabulary of shared values, belief systems fundamental to the growth of human civilization?

Science can tell us about the knowable. It is of little help in the realm of the unknowable or the spiritual. The teachings of virtually all religions are beliefs. All of God's words from whatever revelation have been written and interpreted by men. These are things we believe because we want and need to believe something. They are unarguable because they are unknowable, all save one immutable moral law.

All except the "Golden Rule." "So always treat others as you would like them to treat you; that is the meaning of the Law and the Prophets." (Matthew 7:12)

If I give to you the same opportunity, the same justice, the same treatment that I would have for myself, then you and I can coexist and cooperate. If I demand more than I am willing to give, then one of two things is true. If I am endowed to be superior to you and you accept that position, then we can live in harmony. More likely... if you do not accept my superiority we then live in a chaotic and coercive world where each of us takes what we can by whatever means available.

The golden rule is the necessary and sufficient foundation for civil law and civil society. This is "the meaning of the Law and the Prophets." Beyond this, spiritual beliefs or beliefs about unknowable things are individual choices. A true subscriber to the golden rule, no matter what his or her other beliefs would not contest others making their own choices about what they believe. This leads to two simple conclusions.

Any religion or system of beliefs without the golden rule at its core is in its nature corrupt and despotic.

Beyond that single qualification, anyone who would debase the spirituality or spiritual beliefs of others is as ignorant and unknowing as those he or she would debase.

Sanctimony

Consider the following five organizations: first, a non-profit striving to improve literacy, second a small company specializing in "green" products, third a very profitable multi-national bank, fourth a church and finally a government agency.

Which one of these organizations would you expect to be the best, the most high minded? Which has the greatest impact for good? Which is the most democratic? Which is the most sanctimonious?

If you think you know the answers, from just this brief sketch, perhaps it is you who are most sanctimonious! Every organization must attract investors or donors and satisfy customers. The "best" organization by a democratic standard is the one that pleases customers most, delivers the greatest satisfaction to its investors or donors, does so within the law and thereby lives in greatest harmony within its community. The brief descriptions above give us no useful information to judge any of the organizations by these standards.

Sanctimony is making a claim of moral superiority; it is the placing one's personal or subjective values above those of all others. It is demanding accountability for others while trying to excuse oneself. It is the demeaning of others as corrupt or otherwise below standard, to reduce their credibility and strengthen ones own personal power or influence. It is the vilification as a group of individuals whether they are bankers or oilmen or the press or politicians or lobbyists or any diverse group. It is the "atheist left" condemning the "religious right" as corrupt and destructive, and vice versa.

Sanctimony is an attitude and practice honed over the centuries by kings, tyrants and others who aspire to power. It is driven by the ego, and never a desirable quality in a collaborator or a leader.

Security

In 1962 as a freshly minted engineer I had no idea how lucky I was. Everyone in my class had several very attractive job offers, including some as officers in the military, others in industry with draft deferments, and others with guarantees to hold jobs while they served our country. No one thought of going back to live with parents, or finding a job that would not use all of our skills. None of us had credit cards, much less credit card debt. I had paid my own college expenses and had only $2,000 in tuition loans to pay back. That was more than any of my friends and equal to less than three months pay in my new job.

I took a position with Allis Chalmers in Milwaukee, Wisconsin. After two years I became restless for a new challenge and a new location. I went to Chicago on the Friday after Thanksgiving in 1964 and had two interviews, both of which led to job offers at salaries over 50% above my starting salary less than three years earlier.

My next job was with R. R. Donnelley and Sons Company, the world's largest printer. I started with Donnelley in Chicago in March of 1965. In the lobby of the executive offices was a huge framed register of all Donnelley's 25-year employees. Being somewhat fascinated with numbers I tried to estimate how many of those employed at Donnelley 25 years previously were either still employed there or retired or had died before retirement. My estimate was that between 70 and 80 percent of those working at Donnelley 25 years earlier never subsequently worked anywhere else. That impressed me as a company that offered employment security.

For twenty years, each time I got restless, my bosses gave me a bigger more challenging assignment. I grew, my income grew, and my family grew. Fear or even uneasiness about our future was not part of our vocabulary. In 1985 I was promoted to become a Senior Vice President. Life was good.

Also in 1985 I began to feel a prisoner of my success. Many contemporaries in Donnelley and elsewhere hit walls in their growth, or worse. When "The Company" decides they want you in a lesser role too many had no other options, and their expectations and retirement security took a sharp downturn. My strongest mentors had retired. The company was being run by my generation and each of them had their own trusted cadre. Competition at this level was keen and casualties frequent. I realized that what had seemed to be security was an illusion, that our only real security is the will to control our own destiny.

I began to network, to speak at conferences, to spend more time with customers and suppliers, to look differently at and look for opportunities in the world outside Donnelley. In 1987 a crisis inside Donnelley and an opportunity from outside arrived at the same time. It was a gut wrenching decision, but I left Donnelley. My world was suddenly on its head, and the illusion of security has never returned. Since 1987 I have consulted with printers, publishers, printing technology companies and investors, and have been President of four companies, each needing radical change to survive. It has always been clear that my next paycheck is only as secure as my customer's or my board's current happiness.

This is not just a story of my personal journey. It is also about radical changes in our economy and culture. Competition has become stiffer at every level in every business and in non-profits. In the first decades after World War II Europe and Japan were recovering from devastation and there were no emerging economies. America and American corporations had won the war and profited greatly from the peace. But the rest of the world did recover and began take to their share. By the 1980s, Japan and Europe were ascending. Concurrently, computer networks and personal computers began wiping out entire levels of middle management. Silicon based technology and comprehensive logistics management revolutionized every industry. Every company in America has seen the need to carve 20% or 30% or more of its costs to take advantage of new technologies or succeed against international competitors. Most companies have had to re-invent themselves twice or more in the last two generations. In that environment, the only security for each of us has become the ability and the will to constantly re-invent ourselves. It no longer matters whether we start our careers with the illusion of security. It only matters that we start with vigor and with the knowledge that our destiny is constant change. I am immensely proud that each of my three children successfully re-invented themselves for the first time nearly 10 years earlier in their lives than I did.

The two sectors of our economy that have not yet internalized this reality are government and labor unions. Government departments especially in the federal government are generations behind in the process of re-inventing themselves. Some unions in the private sector have adapted, and many have atrophied or disappeared. Public sector unions are still strong and still largely rooted in the twentieth century. This will change. It will change soon and it will create shock and dismay among many government leaders and employees. This change will be good for us all.

Slavery

In the Ante Bellum south, there were ruthless and cruel slave masters and there were kind and loving slave masters. The difference was not important. The slaves worked each day for the master and at the end of the day took whatever the master gave in return. There was little real happiness.

Too little changed for a century after emancipation. The field slave became a sharecropper and the house slave became a house servant, or worse. The contract and the exploitation were virtually identical. We memorialized in folk tales and songs… "John Henry died with a hammer in his hands." "I load sixteen tons and owe my soul to the company store."

Slavery is the absence of liberty, including but not limited to the right to earn fair wages for ones labor and spend those wages as one pleases. When we ask, "Who sets a fair price for ones labor or property," there are only two possible answers. It can be an agreement between a free buyer and a free seller. Or it can be someone else. We could call that someone else The Master, or we could call it something else without changing the reality.

The communist mantra by Karl Marx, "From each according to his ability, to each according to his needs!" sounds liberating and fair. That is until we ask, "Who determines your abilities and needs?" It has been proven countless times that everyone's ability is diminished without incentives in their self-interest and not everyone can agree on the definition of "needs." Under communism, the dictatorship of the proletariat becomes a dictatorship of the State. The bureaucracy becomes the master. The populace works each day for the State and at the end of the day takes whatever the State gives in return. The populace becomes slaves. There is no liberty, and there has never been a prosperous people without liberty.

Clearly we can assign many roles to the state, including, perhaps especially regulating markets to assure a balance of power between free buyers and free sellers. However, if we allow the state to expand according to the desires of the bureaucracy, it will become the master of all things. How then do we strike a balance, wisely governing the preservation of liberty and fairness? This is perhaps the most important question of our time, yet it is not answerable by any objective maxim or truth. The answer lies in the question at every turn, "Is this expenditure funded by taxes or required by regulation worth the cost it imposes on our liberty to spend our own resources and to regulate our own lives?" The answer also lies in the broader question, "Is the state's protection of the people's liberty commensurate with the liberty it extracts from them via taxes and regulations?"

It is not difficult to see where we are at this moment. Total taxes paid by individuals to all levels of government in the United States are slightly in excess of 30% of their income. Add to that the time and expense to file income taxes, costs to individuals of zoning regulations, building permits, and business licenses. Then add taxes on corporations, additional government borrowings each year and interest on debt we have borrowed. Then add the cost of regulations to banks, safety and environmental regulations, permits to build, operate, expand or export, reporting requirements and certifications for all of the above plus personnel and financial reporting requirements. It is not necessary to conclude that any or all of these taxes and regulations are good or not. Add them together and each of us has surrendered over half of our income, half of our economic liberty to pay for them. We are not free to spend over half of the fruits of our labor because "The State" is spending them. Then consider the nearly $300,000 of debt each on each of our shoulders to liquidate our bonded debt and the unfunded benefits our government has promised.

Vladimir Lenin has been quoted as explaining the totalitarian worldview, "We recognize nothing private!" How far are we today from that vision? Is it not immoral and unfair that all newborn or immigrant Americans begin life here with an indenture of over $300,000 and the prospect receiving, net, less than 50% of what they earn over their lifetime. One does not need to think radically to suggest that every new government expenditure or regulation reaches further into our private domain, or what we once considered personal. Our government has never and will not now voluntarily moderate this overreach. It has become urgent for the electorate to reverse this process toward further enslaving ourselves before it becomes irreversible.

Michael Moffitt

Standards

Every human enterprise needs standards. Families have standards of behavior. Organizations have standard procedures. Industries share standards to facilitate communications and commerce. Nations and civilizations have standards for weights and measures for the same purpose. Standards are different from rules in important ways. Standards must evolve as the world changes. Standards must be built on consensus; they must be beneficial to each user, or they will not be followed and will become less useful to all.

It is exceptionally useful to understand how standards are managed in our increasingly complex world, driven by technology and international trade.

The largest repository of industrial and commercial standards in the world is the American National Standards Institute. Established in 1918, ANSI is a private non-profit organization with the mission: "To enhance both the global competitiveness of U.S. business and the U.S. quality of life by promoting and facilitating voluntary consensus standards and conformity assessment systems, and safeguarding their integrity." Its 3.5 million professional members represent 125 thousand companies, associations and government entities. On it's website it markets published standards from over 180 organizations from the American Boat and Yacht Council to the Wood Machinery Manufacturers Association. ANSI has 90 employees and an annual budget of $22 million.

The largest publisher affiliated with ANSI is ASTM International. ASTM was formed in 1898 by chemists and engineers from the Pennsylvania Railroad. At the time of its establishment, the organization was known as the American Section of the

International Association for Testing and Materials. In 2001, the Society became known as ASTM International.

ASTM publishes and updates over twelve thousand standards serving diverse industries including metals, construction, petroleum, consumer products and many more. When new industries look to advance the growth of cutting-edge technologies, such as nanotechnology and additive manufacturing, many of them come together under the ASTM International umbrella to achieve their standardization goals. Forty six percent of ASTM standards are distributed internationally and 75 countries cite ASTM standards as the basis of national standards.

ASTM has 35 thousand members from 150 countries. It creates and updates standards collaboratively through 142 technical committees. All standards are voluntary. They operate with an annual budget of about $50 million and have an investment fund of $145 million, built up from surplus revenues over the years.

These organizations are models of free enterprise. They are fully supported by their members and customers. They realize the need for thoughtful and flexible standards that lubricate communications throughout commerce and industry. If they create useful standards, their membership applies them and continues to collaborate on new efforts. If their standards do not remain useful, or if they do not adapt as change demands, they will not get applied and membership will loose interest. For over a century they have built collaborative models that perpetuate their usefulness and longevity. They have learned how to maintain a balance between constancy and responsiveness to change.

In 1971 the United States Government created an exceptional case study on the difference between voluntary standards and bureaucratic rule making. The Occupational Health and Safety Administration was established with the mission to "assure safe and healthful working conditions for working men and women by setting and enforcing standards and by providing training, outreach, education and assistance."

At the time ANSI participants had already published over 250 standards related directly to industrial safety. In addition there was a large body of processes and procedures developed by the insurance industry over several decades to help their customers prevent claims for loss or injury. OSHA duplicated and drew from industry and association standards and morphed them into regulations. They instituted no collaborative processes for creating or maintaining standards and fines were and are assessed without due process. OSHA now has an annual budget of $565 million. The OSHA website describes their rulemaking process as taking four and one half to nine years to create and implement each new regulation. In 40 years, through 2011, OSHA has developed no metrics to demonstrate their contribution to industrial safety. During this period, the Department of Justice agreed to prosecute only 51 cases for OSHA and secured 12 misdemeanor convictions for violations. Comparing OSHA to ANSI or their members provides a stark contrast between the cost and effectiveness of self-regulating standards vs. regulations imposed by a remote and self-aggrandizing bureaucracy.

Statistics

When we hear or read any argument supported by a statistic, we should always remember that even the most honest author picks the best possible statistic available to support his or her argument, and presents it in the most convincing way. Statistics can be valuable for analysis and communications, but they can also confuse or mislead.

Seasonal adjustment is a deception used almost exclusively by government statisticians. In business, the manager looks at today vs. one year ago today or this week or month vs. this week or month last year. The data show you are up or down. If down there are no excuses. What must we do to fix the trend? In government we frequently make a complex set of assumptions and "seasonal" adjustments that allow excuses if the numbers don't tell the desired story.

Another favorite is scale. If a monthly number is up two percent and we want it up more, we call it a 24 percent annual rate. If we don't want it up, we just call it two percent up this month. The New York Times and Wall Street Journal both reported a 22.2% drop in military spending in the fourth quarter of 2012. The actual drop for the quarter was 5.3%. Neither story emphasized the note on The Bureau of Economic Analysis source report that, "Percent changes are annualized."

We use a similar technique on graphs. A change from 150 to 160 looks very big if the scale of the graph goes from 145 to 165. A change from 150 to 250 looks very small if the scale is zero to 2000.

Statistics get especially interesting when they are projections. Projections require assumptions that are often hopeful and seldom explicit. At best projections are art, not science. Other times the assumptions can be designed to deceive. For example, the "non-partisan" Congressional Budget Office is required to make projections on the cost of legislation with assumptions dictated within the legislation by its sponsors, whether they believe the assumptions or not.

What is counted in a statistic can be crucial to the apparent story told. It is frequently reported that the US infant mortality rate is the highest in the developed high-income countries of the world. True, but thousands of pre-term babies in other countries are declared stillborn, not included in infant mortality statistics. America's pre-term survival rate is 65% higher than Britain and more than double rates in Finland and Greece where pre term infants are not included infant mortality rates reported to be lower than in the US.

Both of the following statements are true. "The temperature in the contiguous **United States** was the warmest in history in 2012, fully 1 degree F. warmer than the previous record in 1998 and 3.2 degrees F. warmer than the twentieth century average." and

"**World** temperatures moderated slightly in 2012 with cooler average temperatures than all but one year since 2000."

The claim that Medicare has a 2% overhead cost while private health insurance firms have over 20% is frequently stated as fact even though it doesn't pass a cursory smell test. The principal Medicare overhead costs of claims management and collections are handled by Health and Human services and the IRS respectively and not counted in federal accounting as Medicare costs. Secondly, Medicare spends too little overhead to control fraud. Studies by Rand Corporation, Dartmouth, Harvard and others have identified as much as one third of Medicare and Medicaid expenditures to be fraudulent or useless. Why would the 2% overhead rate even come up in an honest conversation?

"Failure rate for AP tests climbing" was a headline for a February, 2010 USA Today story describing performance on advanced placement tests taken by high school juniors and seniors. The percent of students taking the test who received a passing grade of 3 or more on at least one test fell from 65% in 2002 to 60% in 2009. The headline could have read, "Performance on AP tests sharply up!" The story could have focused on the 60% success rate among 800,000 students taking the tests in 2009 vs. a 65% success rate among fewer than 500,000 students taking the tests in 2002. Nearly 500,000 students succeeded in passing AP tests in 2009, up nearly 50% in seven years.

When reading about American education, realize that most statistics about elementary and secondary student performance only include public school students, thus eliminating the 10 percent of all students in private and parochial schools. That may be because government and teacher's unions are not enthusiastic about making those comparisons.

Jobs and employment data are a quagmire. We report them and follow them as though month-to-month changes have meaning. Yet many self employed, voluntary part time workers and people in the cash economy don't get counted. The data are not data, but surveys, and the survey samples do not always meet sound statistical requirements. In 2013 unemployment averaged from 7.6 percent by the narrowest definition to 14.1 percent for all those unemployed who have looked for work in the past twelve months. Unemployment has increased from 2007 rates of 4.5 percent to 8.3 percent for the same range of definitions. All these numbers get quoted in various combinations. What seldom is quoted is that in unadjusted Labor Department and Census numbers from 2007 to 2013 our population increased by 14 million people and employment decreased by nearly four million. To reach the 2007 employment rate of 46.1 percent of the population we need to create nine million new jobs as well as an additional 195 thousand per month to accommodate the growing population. No amount of sugar coating, data adjustments or new presentations will change the reality that we are still sinking behind.

It is seldom explained that the biggest single cause for increasing income disparity among U.S. households is growing income opportunities for women. Think of four people, two doctors and two nurses. In 1980, if these were two couples, they would likely be two male doctors married to two female nurses, two families with approximately equal incomes. Today, because of greater opportunity for women, it would be far more likely to be two doctors, a man and a woman, married to each other and two nurses, a man and a woman, married to each other, creating two families with very different incomes. Substitute executives and analysts or lawyers and paralegals for doctors and nurses and realize that the opportunity for more women to rise to higher income levels is probably the largest single driver for three decades of divergence in household income statistics in America. That is a good thing, not a bad thing.

It is not necessary to go on to make the point. Always look at statistics critically. A statistic that seems too incredible to be true probably isn't. A statistic that seems to make an unbelievable point probably doesn't. This is not new or surprising. The old saw "Figures don't lie, but liars do figure" dates back at least to the nineteenth century.

Stress

Stress can be one of the greatest natural enemies of man. In well-known ways stress leads to heart disease, strokes, overeating and thus obesity and diabetes. It complicates many if not most other diseases. Yet stress is almost entirely self-inflicted.

Reinhold Neiber's famous prayer, "God give me the courage to change what can be changed, the serenity to accept what cannot be changed and the wisdom to know the difference." defines the choice.

We all experience pressure and pain in our lives. In each instance we have options open to us to relieve or to cope with that pressure or pain. Stress is, for the most part, worrying that we cannot change what cannot be changed or punishing ourselves for not changing what can be. Worry is the easy and destructive path. Acceptance of reality and moving on to what can be managed is more productive and tempers stress. Planning and doing is energizing and builds will and confidence. We tell ourselves we are stressed for lack of time, yet we all have the same amount of time each day. We fail to get those things done that we have assigned to a lesser priority.

Stress can also be our great energizer and friend when we dedicate ourselves to a challenging goal. Channeling this stress builds our immune system against external stresses. It uplifts us to extend our possibilities, to reach beyond what we know we can accomplish.

It takes will to pull self out of a picture and see it from the outside. It takes will to apply a symmetrical view to ones own wants or emotions. It takes will to dedicate oneself to a goal and make it happen. Our individual will is the conqueror of stress and the mother of creativity, productivity and serenity. It is not a naïve goal to lead a stress-free life. The principal driver is understanding the distinction between the verbs "to wish" and "to will!"

Subsidiarity

Subsidiarity is a principle of Federalism and an important social teaching of the Roman Catholic Church. The principle is based upon the autonomy and dignity of the human individual, and holds that all forms of society, from the family to the state and the international order, should be in the service of the human person. It holds that all functions of government, business, and other activities should be as local as possible; that government should undertake only those initiatives that exceed the capacity of individuals or private groups acting independently.

The principle of subsidiarity tells us that it is more effective to build our family or business or government with the first principal being the autonomy, wisdom and effectiveness of individuals, and that it is counterproductive to assume the need for central control to micro-manage human activity.

Contrary to this principle it is frequently argued that many functions can be better executed centrally. Ironically those who argue most forcefully in favor of Big Government or Big Labor frequently rant against Big Business "abuses." And vice versa.

It is instructive to think of subsidiarity more broadly and examine natural science and history for clues as to the validity of this principle. Subsidiarity can be defined more broadly as the principle that the sum of outcomes from all the decisions and actions of an autonomous population will produce a far better result than could be accomplished through centralized bureaucratic management.

Adam Smith would agree. The "Invisible Hand" of the market is the sum of all entrepreneurs' efforts to satisfy the needs of all consumers of goods and services. Those who fail to provide value to their customers fail to survive. Those who succeed earn wealth to invest and succeed again. Centrally planned economies have utterly failed to produce employment or wealth or prosperity for all on the scale free market economies have enjoyed.

Darwin would agree. Natural Selection has been a process through which all living species have perfected themselves. Within each of us are thousands of small mutations. These survive through future generations only if beneficial, only if they prove useful. The results are not predictable and sometimes tragic. Yet the total result, the continuous improvement in human performance over our history, is astounding by any measure. Whether we see this process as a manifestation of God's Plan or a sequence of random events, who would bet on a better result from the most brilliant team of human micro-managers?

In addition to its application in natural science, subsidiarity works in the world of industry. The distribution of electric power provides a powerful example. Prior to the first commercial electric motors in 1873, most factories were powered by water or steam engines, with long shafts and belts to drive the looms, lathes, mills, conveyers and other power needs of each factory. With the advent of electric motors, power could be adjacent to many locations. As a result, each machine and each person had more autonomy than before. Each could manage their individual pace. With independence from central mechanical power systems, factories no longer required vertical shafts serving several manufacturing levels to minimize the length of shafts and belts. Architects were liberated to focus design on material flow and to create factories on a single level. Equipment design became focused on function and flexibility rather than conforming to the power source. The transition took more than a half-century.

It was called the second industrial revolution, a period of unprecedented gains in productivity and innovation. Without that transition, it would not have been possible for the United States to convert its entire manufacturing capacity to provide the military power to prevail in WWII. The technology of the electric motor and its application by a multitude of individual enterprises created flexibility and autonomy at every stage in manufacturing industries and that autonomy created the strongest nation on earth. Yet it did not happen via a central plan. It was an incremental process with hundreds of thousands of small innovations by individual entrepreneurs; each building on those that came before.

UNIVAC I, the first commercial computer, was introduced in 1951. The computer revolution and the information age began as a centralized function in every organization. Computers cost millions of dollars. They required a carefully controlled environment and were difficult to use. Electronic calculators began appearing on desktops in the mid 1960s. In 1971, Wang Laboratories introduced the Word Processor. But not until the IBM PC appeared in 1981 did the computer revolution reach individuals and give them flexibility and autonomy. This, and the introduction of the Macintosh in 1984 and Ethernet in 1985 were the real beginnings of the information age. With these new tools for the first time anyone at their desktop could access volumes of information from a centralized data file, use it, reformat it, adapt it, and send it to others.

The greatest impact of this revolution has taken place within the lifetime of nearly everyone in the workforce today! It has affected every aspect of our lives. Organizations have been re-invented. We now have telecommuting, teleconferencing, cell phones, e-mail and the Internet, changing the whole structure of our lives. We don't have as many secretaries, clerks, schedulers, expediters, typesetters, travel agents, telephone operators, bank tellers or messengers. Large corporations have fewer layers of management, because information makes more autonomy possible for everyone. We don't have huge catalogs from Sears, Wards and J.C. Penney, and we have fewer newspapers. Soon we won't have paper telephone directories. This revolution required hundreds of thousands of small innovations over decades; each building on those that came before. The revolution was accelerated by the freedom of every human being to innovate and the discipline of the market as the arbiter of the value of each innovation. There was disruption. Each innovation disrupted many lives, and each of those affected individuals was empowered and responsible to adjust to their new situation and upgrade their skills. During this same period, the fascist world and then the communist world were committed to central planning of investment and innovation. They failed to innovate and to compete, leaving democracies as the primary innovators of the information age.

After each of these processes we find ourselves in a much better world created by an enterprising society with government principally protecting the freedom to do so. Central planners would have been, and in fact were, paralyzed by the fear of unemployment in both the manufacturing and information revolutions. But individuals, one at a time working independently and together, found ways to do things better, faster and more effectively. They found ways to re-train themselves and others with new skills for the new age. When we look at all this experience, it is hard not to admire the creative process driven by a multitude of individual seemingly independent efforts.

Of course progress and change are not without pain. That pain, however, is the price of any change. Just as birth would not be possible without death, we cannot build the new without retiring the old. The greatest enemy of subsidiarity is not that it is an imperfect principal. The enemy is that we often forget how imperfect political and bureaucratic processes are, especially in rigidity and waste created and by failure to deliver innovation. Perhaps President Roosevelt did great damage when, at his 1941 inaugural he told us to expect freedom from want and freedom from fear. These "freedoms" are wonderful sound bites but antithetical to the human condition and destructive to the creative process.

Taxation and Subsidies

There are a few things nearly all Americans agree on. First, our government needs to do some things that our founding fathers never dreamed possible. Second, our nation is so incredibly wealthy that we should be able to assure that even the most inept or disadvantaged in our midst shares this bounty at some level and with some dignity.

We not only agree on these things. We have agreed on them for so long that we have built a maze of subsidies to help most imaginable groups of the "disadvantaged." This patchwork is so pervasive and complex that it is impossible to measure or even define success or failure. We have federal subsidies and grants and aid for family and corporate farmers, for homeowners, college students, the elderly, the unemployed, the disabled, small businesses, minority businesses, local governments and the full range of non-profit organizations. Programs for the poor subsidize food, medical care, housing and day care. Hundreds of programs, each staffed by thousands of bureaucrats, each help some group, miss some deserving individuals, serve to distort markets, distort income statistics and each has the potential for and reality of abuse.

Nearly everyone also agrees that our income tax system is a convoluted mire. If we could start over, would we do things differently? Would we try to help the disadvantaged more efficiently and give them more freedom to select how they are helped? Would we try to craft a simpler and more manageable tax code? It is unfathomable that leaders with honorable intentions cannot even engage in a serious conversation about a new direction. If this failure continues, we are surely doomed to be paralyzed by our past.

In 1968, Milton Friedman suggested a negative income tax as a less intrusive approach to federal welfare. That idea has never gained traction, but it is a better idea today and available funds are clearly not the problem. In 2013 our federal government spent $820 billion on subsidies to individuals for disability and unemployment benefits, Medicaid, housing, food and public assistance benefits. With these funds we could give every man woman and child in our population a tax credit, a negative tax of $3,300 per year if we reduced the credit to an individual up to any Social Security pensions and taxed Social Security benefits as ordinary income. (You will see below that this tax would only affect some of the top 40 percent of incomes.) This level of subsidy would cost no more than existing fragmented subsidies even if we left all the current bureaucracies in place.

According to the National Commission on Fiscal Responsibility and Reform (Simpson Bowles), appointed by President Obama, if we eliminated all deductions for mortgage interest, state and local taxes, charitable giving and other "tax expenditures" we could fund a $3,300 per man woman and child flat income tax deduction. There are many possibilities, but think for a moment of the impact of two such reforms, a $3,300 tax credit and a $3,300 tax exemption for every man woman and child, coupled with a 30 percent flat tax rate.

- Every single individual who finds work for 24 hours per week at eight dollars per hour would pass to the positive side of the single person poverty guidelines.
- Every two-person household with a $6,600 tax credit and a $6,600 exemption and one person working 24 hours each week at eight dollars per hour would have household income above the poverty guideline.

- A family of four would pay no payroll taxes and would use their tax credit to pay all income taxes until their income reached $57,200 annually.
- Federal personal income tax receipts would increase from current levels and would be paid entirely by households with *per capita* incomes greater than $14,300. Even though the tax rate is flat, the least prosperous 40 percent of households would pay no tax and 80 percent of the revenue would come from the 20 percent of households with the greatest incomes. This works because those in the middle no longer subsidize mortgages, local taxes and charitable giving for those who are better off.
- It also helps to realize that a reduced rate on capital gains and dividends is a subsidy to those who trade capital at the expense of those who earn income through their skills and labor. Why should we think that income from the sale of an investment of six months duration is somehow different or more desirable or will be spent differently than income from the annual return on that investment or from our labor?
- Additional bureaucratic cost savings would be at least in the tens of billions in departments like HUD, Agriculture, IRS, and HHS. More important, perhaps most important the power to interfere with the lives of our citizens would be stripped from these bureaucracies. Those who are less fortunate would gain financial resources and the power and freedom to spend or invest them according to their judgment. Who but the most arrogant of bureaucrats would claim to know needs of citizens never encountered and how to make rules to satisfy those needs better than the citizens themselves.

No doubt some will aptly observe that this sort of reform will not end all human misery, nor will it satisfy the need for personally delivered assistance from private organizations and states and municipalities. But the example shows that the money is available to end poverty as we currently define it for all households in which one person could find employment at minimum wage for twenty-four hours per week. It can end poverty in a way that respects the dignity of every citizen, does not dictate each family's priorities or choices and does not distort markets by bureaucratic fiat. The tax credit may be perceived as a "government dole", but it encourages citizens to earn their way out of the dole. There are no penalties for moving into the productive economy. For the first dollars earned, the citizen keeps the entire value. Once the threshold of poverty is reached, the citizen will still always keep 70 percent of everything he or she earns.

Many should and will no doubt question the details or the numbers. The example illustrates what can be done with money we now spend. It does not illustrate the only possibility. So long as we really make the tax credit and deduction a replacement for micro-managed subsidies and their supporting bureaucracies, the numbers will work easily. The details of special human cases can and should be dealt with by states, municipalities and private charities. There, people in contact with needs and local conditions, can count on the tax credit as a floor under services to be provided by local human hands. If we are disciplined about replacement of the current subsidy mire, the numbers can be adjusted over time based on what we need and can afford, but the unburdened subsidy will always cost less than the burdened one.

Two underlying principles are far more important than the specifics of the illustration. First, fixing our regimen of taxation and subsidies cannot be accomplished by adding more complexity.

More complexity and micromanagement will create higher bureaucratic costs, abuse and market distortion and will not improve more lives.

Second, government bureaucracies are in their nature driven by inflexible rules and the power to enforce them. Charity should be driven by caring and giving and human flexibility. The two are fundamentally incompatible. We have seen the result in government becoming increasingly abusive and manipulative as it tries to micro-manage the lives of the poor. It is a core principle of any free society that every citizen, rich or poor, must strive to become a responsible adult. If we convert whatever subsidies we can afford into a cash tax credit, who knows how many "poor" will use that freedom to lift themselves and their families, as did most of our ancestors? Should we not give them a boost rather than a leash?

Time

Carpe Diem translates as "Seize the Day!" I prefer to think of it more as "Seize the Moment!" For we live in moments. Each day is an accumulation of many moments, and we can only grasp each moment in that moment.

Why is it that we are directed to seize each moment, and to what purpose? Seizing the moment is only useful in our lives if we not only grasp the moment but also direct it to a purpose. Moments are the core ingredient of our lives. Each moment can be spent only once, and then it is gone. If it was not spent to improve our life, then it was wasted, causing our life to be less than it might have been.

It is very irksome to be told, "I'm sorry, I didn't have time for this…. Or that!" We all have the same number of moments in each day. We choose to use each according to our own priorities and purposes. If we don't get to this or that, it is never because we did not have time. It is because we had other priorities, we used our time toward another purpose, or lacking another purpose we chose to waste those moments. To "Seize the Moment!" is to be in control of one's life, to be the director and executor of our own existence, to choose the purpose of each moment and thus take responsibility for the fullness of our life.

We should always take care not to confuse "Carpe Diem! with "Diem Carpe!" Seizing the moment is the antithesis of being seized by events. It is very easy to be captured by the thrill of the rapids and come to believe we are in control of the kayak. Seizing the moment is deciding on what stream to travel, when to get into the kayak and when to get out. Being seized by the moment is becoming so absorbed in the rapids that we forget to or are unable to get to or to get out at our chosen destination.

Vertical Pronoun (The)

My father drummed into my young brain to be wary of the vertical pronoun. "I think this…" No one cares. "I want that…" No one cares. "I am the greatest!" No one agrees. He taught me to read a letter or a treatise and excise all the vertical pronouns. He gave me forever a consciousness that it is almost never convincing to lead with the "I" word!

It is instructive to read any document, written by self or other, and count the vertical pronouns. The more "I"s, the more the author is focused on self and the less focused on the audience. The more "I"s; the more arrogance. It is a wonderful discipline to remove the "I" word from your vocabulary, and always focus on the "you." Regardless if you are speaking with a student, a teacher, a leader, a follower, an antagonist, a customer, a friend or a lover, when you stand in the shoes of one with whom you would communicate or persuade, you never see or say "I!"

Victims

On Halloween night 2008 Bryshon Nellum a nineteen year old USC track star was shot in both legs on a Los Angeles street. It took three surgeries to remove the shotgun pellets and repair the damage. With the third operation, he risked his ability to walk in order to regain his opportunity to run.

After four years of surgeries, rehab and concentrated training, on August 10, 2012, Nellum and the American team won a Silver Medal in the 4 x 400 yard relay at the London Olympics.

In 2008, Nellum could have considered himself a victim, and indeed he was. Yet, he refused to accept "victimhood." He could have easily accepted disability, yet he chose to compete.

My friend Walter was born in New Orleans in 1935. He was a handsome black man with few advantages. The assets he remembers most are his grandmother, "Mama Rose," always with a homespun cliché about hard work, honesty and self-reliance, and the love of his beautiful Ursula. Walter and Ursula were married in 1954. They had seven children and Walter supported the family for many years as a soft drink delivery truck driver. All seven of their children went to and graduated from college. Two sons started an audio-visual equipment company serving meetings and conventions. Another son is a policeman, another a fireman. Two daughters worked for the City of New Orleans and another for a bank.

I first met Walter in 1994. His job as a delivery driver had evaporated in a consolidation of bottlers. He was working as a courier and handyman for Century Graphics when I came to manage the company. He retired in 2000 at age 65, living comfortably even if as a poverty statistic. His Social Security plus income from part time work as a handyman and gardener yielded as much as his income before retirement. His children bought him a new car and with no mortgage or rent, Walter and Ursula viewed their life as good.

I was privileged to join Walter and Ursula, their entire family and a few friends to celebrate their 50th wedding anniversary and re-commitment of vows in the spring of 2004. By this time they had 17 grandchildren, the two oldest already in college at LSU. The whole family, all in suits and best dresses sang hymns of praise with great feeling and respect.

Near the end of the evening I asked Walter if he could possibly have dreamed of this occasion 50 years earlier. He could only shake his head in awe of his miracle.

On August 29, 2005, Walter unwisely chose to stay home during hurricane Katrina. He was rescued by boat from his house before it became completely submerged. From the boat to the high-rise overpass and then to San Antonio, Walter traveled as a refugee. It was his first time to fly both in a helicopter and an airplane. He had lost everything except the clothes on his back. By September 13 Walter had connected with Ursula and a daughter and grandson and he tried to call me, leaving a despondent message. On September 20 when we finally connected Ursula had an apartment in San Antonio, daughter Lissy had a job there; ("She can do anything." Walter said proudly.) Walter, back in New Orleans, had already rummaged through the ruins of their home for a few keepsakes. Two sons had also lost homes but there was insurance and the family was accounted for and uninjured, ready together for their next chapter.

Today, Walter and Ursula live in a newer neighborhood in a renovated and raised house, statistically in poverty, yet still surrounded by family solidly in the "middle class."

There is no question that Walter and Ursula and their children and their grandchildren were and are victims of discrimination. Nor is there any question that they live their lives with great and justified pride. Walter and Ursula started out with little opportunity and made much of it. They never let victimhood govern or depreciate their lives. When Walter is asked, "How is your day going?", he still quotes Mama Rose, "You gotta take the bitter with the sweet!"

It has become epidemic in our culture to create large envelopes for victims and to spend great resources to include as many as possible in these envelopes. We do it in class action suits where the goal is to get the most money by defining as many as possible as within the "class". We do in diagnosing disabilities. One in ten of our population between ages six and twenty-one is classified as disabled according to the Americans with Disabilities Education Act. We do it in affirmative action, where all in a race or gender are assumed to need or deserve an affirmative action advantage. We consider it improper to be exclusionary in any "entitlement" program.

Each of us, and our society will be stronger when we realize the great wisdom of Bryshon and Walter. If we teach our children that they are victims of a discrimination or disability or of any adversity, they will believe us, and accept "victimhood." If we teach them to focus on their abilities, and their responsibility to manage whatever adversity they face, they will believe us and take charge of their own lives. If we teach them that every person is different, stronger in some ways than in others, we can then teach them that success is being the best you can be and failure is guaranteed by playing the victim. If we really believe that one in ten of our children and young adults should be designated as "disabled" and that the 20% of us with the least are "disadvantaged," how can we hope for them to be heroes?

As a child and teenager, whenever I complained to my father about misfortune or injustice, his invariable response was that I should look in the mirror. If I forgot why, he would explain (again): "If you blame someone else for your problems then you have no power to fix them." In any situation, only if I would look in the mirror and accept responsibility could I then take charge of the solution. If I was getting beaten up, I should become stronger. If I wanted something, I should find a way to earn it. If I got a poor grade, I should study harder. If I had an accident that wasn't my fault, I should have been watching out for the "other guy"! This at the time seemed a singularly unsympathetic view, but it has served me well.

Being a hero, or a victim is not about the cards you are dealt. It is much more about who you are and what you do with those cards.

Acknowledgements

No work can be done without supporters and mentors. *Granddad's Dictionary* is no exception. My sister Suzie McDonald was my first critic and offered great encouragement. Elizabeth Eulberg, an accomplished author in her own right also offered encouragement and valuable guidance. My wife Brenda has been my greatest fan and a most wonderful editor. I must also give great credit to Westbow Publishing for their business model. They call it self-publishing, but offer many services of both publishers and agents and they do so with great professionalism.

It would be impossible to list all those who contributed to my education, the learning that enabled this book. The beginning was of course my parents Marion and Roy, to whom this book is dedicated. Not enough can be said of what they gave to me. My three best friends in college, Allen Gibbs, Peter Smith and Phil Turner were there when many of the ideas in the book were embryos, and also became my first lasting friends. In my business career, the most important people were the many who worked for and with me, helping me to learn, grow and accomplish many goals. In this great army I found my optimism. Nearly all were honest, hard working, dedicated to their families and to whatever they committed their energy. This experience makes it impossible for me to judge any diverse group of people as being otherwise.

A few leaders and teachers made huge investments in my growth. Jim Wentworth and George Teller, my first bosses at Allis Chalmers gave me my head and their confidence, and first taught me the fun of business. At R. R. Donnelley, Gordon Ewing, Bill Laichas and Don Reeves all did the same. Jim Bickers stands the tallest among all my Donnelley mentors with his complete dedication to perfecting my skills and my understanding of selling, of organizations and power. George Sacerdote taught me the consulting business at A. D. Little. Kip Colwell at Banta Corporation and Jon Newcomb at Simon and Schuster were wonderful clients, each giving me opportunities to shape the transition of the printing and publishing industries. Terry Daniels, the Managing Partner and guru of Quad-C made a huge bet, funding the buyout of Century Graphics, and he was the best possible counselor in making that bet pay off.

If we listen, our wives should be our most important teachers. Ann and I had 36 years before she was taken away. It is impossible to count all we shared including what she gave our children and the balance she gave our lives. Brenda and I have shared only six years, but she too has made me the luckiest man alive.

CPSIA information can be obtained at www.ICGtesting.com
Printed in the USA
LVOW12s0840180414

382152LV00002B/3/P